On Grades and Grading

Supporting Student Learning through a More Transparent and Purposeful Use of Grades

Timothy Quinn

ROWMAN & LITTLEFIELD EDUCATION
A division of
ROWMAN & LITTLEFIELD PUBLISHERS, INC.
Lanham • New York • Toronto • Plymouth, UK

Published by Rowman & Littlefield Education
A division of Rowman & Littlefield Publishers, Inc.
A wholly owned subsidiary of The Rowman & Littlefield Publishing Group, Inc.
4501 Forbes Boulevard, Suite 200, Lanham, Maryland 20706
www.rowman.com

10 Thornbury Road, Plymouth PL6 7PP, United Kingdom

British Library Cataloguing in Publication Information Available

Library of Congress Cataloging-in-Publication Data

Quinn, Timothy.
On grades and grading : supporting student learning through a more transparent and purposeful use of grades / Timothy Quinn.
pages cm
Includes bibliographical references and index.
ISBN 978-1-61048-911-9 (cloth : alk. paper) -- ISBN 978-1-61048-912-6 (pbk. : alk. paper) -- ISBN 978-1-61048-913-3 (electronic)
1. Grading and marking (Students) I. Title.
LB3051.Q57 2013
371.27'2--dc23
371.27'2--dc23

∞™ The paper used in this publication meets the minimum requirements of American National Standard for Information Sciences Permanence of Paper for Printed Library Materials, ANSI/NISO Z39.48-1992.

Printed in the United States of America

To Todd Eckerson—
for inspiring me to learn
and then inspiring me to teach.

Grades are not about what students earn;
they are about what students learn.

—*Susan Brookhart*

Contents

Contents

Preface

This book represents the thoughts of one educator, developed over more than a decade of work as a classroom teacher. I am confident that this book provides food for thought and I hope it will encourage educators at all levels to reflect seriously and purposefully on how and why they assign grades. It is my further hope that this book will provide insights that spur change in classrooms across the country.

The ideas contained in this book stem from my own experience combined with a great deal of reading and thinking about education. I welcome researchers and theorists inspired by these ideas to conduct the studies necessary to establish a more definitive and data-driven understanding of best practices in grading, one that will better support student learning.

Introduction

OVERVIEW

As the title suggests, this book examines the nature of grades, the process through which they are determined, and their relationship to student learning.

Part 1 of this book is theoretical. The two chapters in this section take a careful look at the many ways in which grades can be defined and the different purposes that grades can serve. This includes an analysis of the ways in which the different definitions and purposes affect student learning in different ways. While part 1 is almost entirely theoretical, it provides an essential underpinning for all that follows, as the practical specifics of grading should not be considered before one has carefully defined what a grade means and determined for what purposes it will be used.

Part 2 is much more practical. It examines a number of complicated issues related to grading and provides overviews and analyses of different approaches to grading, looking carefully at the intended and unintended effects of specific grading systems and policies. While the chapters in part 2 occasionally draw upon one another, teachers and administrators need not read them in order, and can pick and choose based upon issues that concern them and their schools.

This book provides strategies and suggestions for teachers and administrators in the hope that evaluating assignments and giving out report cards will become more meaningful gestures—gestures that support and enhance student learning, as opposed to actions that merely comment upon student learning. This book should also serve as an important reference for students and parents who wish to be better informed about the ways in which academic performance is quantified, symbolized, described, evaluated, and ranked.

LINKING GRADES TO LEARNING

Because grades send powerful messages about learning and achievement, messages that can have a significant impact on the lives of students, grading has become an extremely complicated and controversial topic in education. Hence, as educators, we must think carefully about the nature and purpose of our grading systems and closely examine their effect on student learning.

We must ask of our grading systems and policies what we should ask of all policies in our schools—do they inhibit or support student learning, and if they support it, how can this support be enhanced? The purpose of this book is to help educators more effectively confront this question and to provide them with the knowledge and strategies needed to improve their grading systems and policies.

Initially, this book intended simply to examine issues related to grading without offering a particular point of view. However, working from the premise that grades—like all elements of education—should be used to support student learning, it became impossible not to develop a particular perspective. The reader will see this perspective emerge implicitly and explicitly over the course of the book. There are many possibilities for what grades can be, many purposes they can serve, and many ways in which they can be determined, but this does not mean that all grading systems are equal.

Nevertheless, it remains true that there is no one right way to grade and no single answer to what makes the best grading system and policy. Although a point of view will become clear, it consists of guidelines and principles, not specific mandates. Thus, it remains up to individual teachers and schools to determine what the most appropriate grading systems and policies are for their particular students. The specifics may change depending upon the particular mission, values, and goals of the teachers and schools, but what must not change is the underlying idea that grading systems and policies must be in the service of student learning.

This book portrays certain systems of grading in a more favorable light than others; however, more important than its arguments for the use of particular grading systems is the book's call to educators to be more transparent and more purposeful in their use of grades.

WHY GRADES CAN SEEM ARBITRARY AND MEANINGLESS

Before turning to an examination of grades and the grading process, let us first consider why it is that students and teachers often feel negatively about both. While they may be very concerned with them, most students dislike grades: they provoke anxiety, cause stress, and are often—at least from the vantage point of the student—regarded as unfair.

Although students may think their teachers relish the opportunity to pass judgment upon them and their work, many teachers actually do not enjoy giving grades, and one would be hard pressed to find a teacher who enjoys grading. In fact, grading can be the bane of a teacher's existence, so much so that it alone has driven teachers from a profession that they otherwise enjoyed. Teachers will commonly list grading as the least meaningful and most tiresome element of their job and would generally prefer to avoid it. In the old joke about grading, a teacher throws tests down a flight of stairs and grades them based on where they land.

In a promotional clip for the Canadian Broadcasting Company sitcom *Mr. D*, the teacher whose name gives the show its title articulates a more "nuanced" approach to grading while he and his friend sit at a bar looking at a stack of papers:

Friend: There goes your weekend, eh? Marking.

Mr. D: No, not really. Let me explain how this works. If these were regular tests, what I would do is I would find the smartest student's, Maya, and I would mark hers first. And I would use that as my answer key. But these are essay questions. Now, if I were to read these, it would take forever. So I don't. So I look at their mark going into it, okay, like Maya. [She] has the highest mark in the class. There she is. So that's my answer key.

Friend: Don't you already know the answers?

Mr. D: Sometimes theirs are better. I gotta give her a good mark. Couple circles, and then sometimes, [writes] "too vague," "too vague." That way I don't have to give her a hundred.

Friend: Yeah, keep it realistic.

Mr. D: They only look at the mark—96. I give her a little more than she has going in. That way she won't come back and challenge me. Okay?

Friend: That's a good system.

Mr. D then moves on to his lower-performing students:

Mr. D: Jimmy, Jimmy, look at Jimmy. [Showing paper] Nothing, nothing, garbage, waste of time. 33. There's some words there, but I have no time to read them. So then I get angry. [Writes] "Jimmy, ridiculous, this has got to stop."

Friend: He could say the same thing about you.

With another low-performing student, his friend offers a more empathetic suggestion:

Mr. D: Okay, here's Mike. Now Mike's got a 62.

Friend: You should give him an 80.

Mr. D: [Snaps fingers] Give 'em an 80.

Friend: That'll make his day.

Mr. D: Make his day. And he goes home. His parents are excited. I like that.

Friend: Like you've been rooting for him the whole time.

Mr. D: [Writes] "Finally . . . about time . . . thank you."

Yet Mr. D's more malicious side creeps back in:

Mr. D: Now this person, Shawna—I don't like her. She drives me nuts. So what I do is I fail her on the exam but I just give her enough to pass the course so I don't have to teach her again. Check marks, some question marks, underline some things, couple good comments . . .

Friend: Mediocre.

Mr. D: Haven't used that one, that's a good one. [Writes] "Happy face, smile."

Friend: That's, ah . . . disturbing.[1]

Now, this depiction of the grading process is an extreme parody, one that will undoubtedly offend the many teachers who take the grading process far more seriously. However, although not quite as self-serving or deceitful, a less extreme form of this parody probably happens more often than educators would like to admit, giving credence to student complaints that grades are arbitrary and unfair.

Why would a teacher approach grading in this manner? Is it simply because the amount of work involved is so daunting? Perhaps in some cases, but more often it can be because the work of grading feels like a meaningless task—procedural work that is completely removed from the actual process of teaching and learning.

Granted, students take their grades seriously, but only because of the perceived impact of grades on their future. Students do not necessarily find grades relevant to learning and generally care about little other than what tangible benefit they may receive from earning certain grades. Students do not perceive a genuine link between grades and learning, and hence, teachers employ grading systems that do not support learning or give little effort to producing grades that are relevant to and useful in the learning process.

Thus, in the worst cases, a self-perpetuating cycle is created—one in which the connection between grades and learning becomes less and less clear: teachers do not give useful and relevant grades, so students do not put any stock in them as tools to greater learning. Because of this, teachers put less thought and effort into the grading process, and students respond accordingly. This pattern continues on and on until neither party believes grades are related to learning, and we end up—at least in the public mind—with the grading system of Mr. D.

WHY GRADES ACTUALLY ARE MEANINGFUL

It's understandable that, at least from a pedagogical standpoint, grading might seem to be a rather inconsequential topic. After all, grading generally happens after the teaching and learning have occurred, which can perhaps lead one to conclude that grades have no impact on either of these processes. If this were, in fact, the case, grading would not be worthy of much study, other than to figure out methods of doing it more efficiently. However, the process of (1) evaluating a student's work on a given task, (2) assigning that work a grade, and then (3) determining some form of summative grade that is an aggregate of multiple grades over a period of time can actually have far-reaching consequences for learning.

There are three general ways in which grades can have an impact on learning:

1. Grades can provide data upon which to base decisions.
2. Grades can have a tremendous impact on student motivation.
3. Grades can provide students with important feedback on their work.

Data-based decision making, increased student motivation, and more relevant, specific, and useful feedback can all lead to greater learning, and it is upon this standard that the efficacy of any grading system and policy should be judged.

There may be other considerations that one can bring to a discussion of grading, but they generally pertain to the sorting and ranking of students for nonpedagogical purposes. These considerations—about who gets accepted to which school and who gets which job offer—are not educational per se. Yes, colleges and employers desire data about their applicants, but the purpose of schools is not to serve the needs of colleges and employers; it is to educate students.

Thus, educators should not concern themselves with the sorting and ranking of students. Various constituencies in our society may desire and, in fact, require this sorting and ranking, but it is not the job of schools to provide this service. By all means, colleges and employers should have access to student grades, but the ease with which our grading systems allow these groups to sort and rank students should not be a driving concern for schools.

In examining grading systems or policies, the prominent considerations should be (1) whether or not they provide useful data upon which to make pedagogical and curricular decisions; (2) whether or not they appropriately motivate students; and (3) whether or not they provide students with relevant, useful, and specific feedback on their work—three things that didn't seem to have concerned Mr. D at all.

We are a nation addicted to grades, and we are obsessed with them for all of the wrong reasons. So let us try to channel this addiction to grades in a positive direction; let us try to transform it into something else—an addiction to learning.

NOTE

1. Jerry Dee and Michael Volpe, *Mr. D*, Canadian Broadcasting Company, video, 2:01, December 16, 2011, http://www.youtube.com/watch?v=0fn_vAhu_Lw. Quoted with permission from the executive producers.

Part 1

Grades: Definitions and Purposes

Chapter 1

Grades Defined

BRINGING MEANING TO THE MEANINGLESSNESS

Think carefully about the statements below:

- Mr. Smith is an easy grader.
- An A should only be for a grade of 92 and above.
- There's no way half of our students should be earning grades of B or better.
- "How can Katie be on the honor roll when she has a C in one of her classes?
- C isn't an average grade anymore.
- Mrs. Jones is so unfair—only one student earned high proficiency on the project!
- I, like, totally failed that test!

One hears comments like these in the halls of schools every day, and generally, no one pays them any mind. But, in actuality, they should make you scratch your head, because without clear definitions of the different grades referenced in them, they are essentially meaningless.

A teacher puts an A on a paper. What does that mean? A student gets 75 percent of the questions on a quiz right, so he earns a C. Why? A parent is ecstatic because her child's overall average has gone up two points. Is that really a big deal? A teacher curves the scores on a test so that the grades fit a bell curve. Is that fair? One administrator is dismayed that the average grade for a course seems to be getting higher every year. Another administrator is pleased that student performance is on the rise. What's the difference?

Clearly, before evaluating whether or not various grading systems and policies support student learning, we need to define our grades. This process starts by drawing some important distinctions.

IMPORTANT DISTINCTIONS: ASSESSMENT, EVALUATION, AND GRADES

Over the past decade, much ink has been spilled on the topic of assessment. Theorists, researchers, teachers, and administrators have worked tirelessly to devise tools for measuring student learning in an accurate, fair, and authentic manner—one that promotes as well as measures learning. Educators are correct to spend so much time thinking about, writing about, and experimenting with assessment, for what we assess and how we assess send powerful messages to students about what we value and can have a significant impact on student learning.

However, the terms *assessment* and *assess* can be confusing, particularly when used in conjunction with the terms *grade* and *grading*. In the field of education, the term *assessment* is most often used as a noun referring to the actual tasks that teachers have students complete in order to display their learning. On the other hand, we have the verb *assess*, which means to evaluate and respond to a student's performance on a given task. Two synonyms for the verb *assess* are the words *evaluate* and *grade*. This creates more confusion since *grade* can be a noun referring to the label placed upon a student's work.

In order to avoid confusion, this book distinguishes between these terms in the following manner. *Assessment* is used as a noun to refer to a tool used to measure student learning and eventually to generate grades. *Grades* themselves are labels placed upon student work that are determined through a process of *evaluation*. It is this process to which the noun *grading* refers. The focus of this book, then, is on that process (grading) and the labels that it produces (grades).

Another way in which to understand these distinctions is by thinking about how they work together as a multistep process.

1. The teacher gives an assessment.
2. The teacher engages in the grading process, evaluating the student's work on the assessment.
3. The teacher responds to the work by assigning a grade to it.

Then there is actually a fourth step that concludes the process:

4. The teacher reports this grade in some form to the appropriate parties.

While these steps may be combined, if one really breaks the process down, one will see that each step genuinely represents a distinctive action. Regardless, it is steps 2–4 that educators are referring to when they talk about grading, and this must be distinguished from what educators generally refer to as assessment.

Keep in mind that this process refers only to the grading of a specific assessment task and not to the determination of some form of summative grade. That process is examined later in the book, and it is even more complicated since it entails finding a meaningful and accurate way to combine multiple grades on individual assessments.

One may argue that grading is simply one element of the larger concept of assessment. While perhaps this is true, the distinction is important because of how frequently the term *assessment* is used only to refer to the tasks that students are asked to complete rather than the evaluation of, response to, and reporting about student work.

Hence, with all of the thought given to methods of assessment, what has perhaps not received sufficient attention in the educational literature is methods of evaluating, responding to, and reporting student performance on assessments. Although assessment and grading are inextricably linked to one another, they are not the same thing, and conflating the two terms does not allow educators to do justice to the topics of grades and grading. This book is an attempt to remedy this situation.

WHAT ARE GRADES?

Grades are loosely defined above as a "label placed upon student work," but a more precise definition is needed. One needs to be more specific about what exactly a grade is meant to represent.

Let us start with the most general definition of a grade possible and then work from there:

> A grade is a piece of information that attempts to report something about a student's education.

Quite vague, isn't it? The reason it is so vague is that a grade can represent so many different things, and to be any more specific would inevitably exclude a possible type of grade.

Consider Table 1.1, which outlines the numerous possibilities and combinations for the three parts of the definition. Items in each column of the table can be aligned with any of the elements in the other two columns, yielding the following generic template for a definition of a grade:

> "A grade is a _____ of _____ relative to _____."

As one can see from Table 1.1, coming up with a more precise definition for grades is not quite as simple as it might first seem.

Table 1.1

Type of Information	Topic of Information	Context for Information
A grade is a/an . . .	*of . . .*	*relative to . . .*
Quantification	A student's learning	A standard
Symbol	A student's skill level at a certain time	A student's peers within a class, school, grade, or age level in a particular region
Description	A student's average skill level over a period of time	A student's starting point
Evaluation	A student's performance on an individual assessment task	All other possible outcomes
Ranking	A student's performance on a number of assessment tasks	
	A student's progress over a certain period of time	

In certain cases, the third component of this definition template will not be necessary. It also should be noted that Table 1.1 may not be exhaustive. It is the template that matters, and individuals should fill in the blanks as they see fit.

Leaving aside what specific form a grade takes (number, letter, etc.—there is much discussion of this later), in order to determine the type of information a grade represents, one must ask what it is doing: quantifying, symbolizing, describing, evaluating, or ranking?

This leads to the question of what is being quantified, symbolized, described, evaluated, or ranked. Is it a student's learning, a student's skill level at a particular time, a student's average skill level over a period of time, a student's performance on an individual assessment task, a student's performance on a number of assessment tasks, or a student's progress over a certain period of time?

Finally, one must consider the context for the information. Is this piece of information meant to be relative to a standard, relative to others in a class, school, or grade level, relative to an individual student's starting point, or simply relative to all other possible outcomes?

It may seem as though much of this is splitting hairs, but if you look closely, you will see that many of these descriptors have important nuances—seemingly small distinctions that have widely different implications. If grades do have an enormous impact on student learning, then these distinctions can become very significant.

Thus, we will now look closely at each of these three components that make up the definition of a grade.

The Type of Information

To determine the type of information provided by a grade, we must examine the subtle but significant distinctions between the different things a grade can do. These distinctions may lead naturally to different forms that a grade might take. Both of these things—what a grade is doing and what form it takes—have significant implications that must be considered carefully.

First, grades can quantify, which clearly suggests that a grade will be numerical in form. Depending on the range in which the number falls, it can lead to different interpretations. If the numbers are assigned on a scale of 0–100, then they imply a percentage of material correct, although not all assignments can be evaluated in this manner. If the numbers are between 0 and 4, they imply a traditional letter grading system with the numbers corresponding to certain letters (generally A–F), which would themselves need to be defined.

From this, one can begin to see that grades as quantifications may be problematic, since much of the information that grades attempt to report is difficult to quantify. The one exception, again, is when a teacher is reporting a percentage of correct material on an assessment, but it seems that this is limited to only certain types of assessments, which are used less and less frequently given current educational practices that encourage more open-ended and authentic assessments. Even if one uses some assessments that can be graded with a percentage, how should one combine that with an assessment that is scored more holistically in order to determine a summative grade? (A more complete analysis of number grades can be found in chapter 4.)

The next thing that grades can do is act as symbols. Symbols can be similar to quantifications; in fact, quantifications are simply a very specific type of symbol. In using the term *symbol*, though, we open up a greater range of possibility for the form a grade may take. Letter grades are surely the most common system of symbols. Yet, whether the symbols are A, B, and C, or smiley faces and frowns, they are merely symbols standing for something else. Hence, one needs to be made aware of what they symbolize by linking them to something more specific, be it a standard of performance or some other descriptor. In any case, symbols open up a greater range of possibility than quantifications, yet they are limited in terms of the amount of information that they can provide and must rely on a clear connection to what they are meant to symbolize in order to be meaningful.

Whereas quantifications and symbols are similar, those concepts differ greatly from a grade as a description. A description suggests that specific and detailed information will be supplied, and while quantifications and symbols can be linked to generic descriptors, they provide very little in the way of specific details. Furthermore, they do not allow teachers to distinguish between students earning the same grade, despite the fact that there will be countless differences between two students who earn the symbol B. Grades as descriptions must be narrative in form, and, given the amount of time and effort narrative reporting requires, it is no wonder that grades come more commonly in the form of quantifications or symbols, despite the fact that the latter two provide less useful information.

The next type of grade is an evaluation. An evaluation differs from the previous three types (quantification, symbol, and description) because it implies a judgment. While the previous three can be used as evaluations, they need not be used in that way, as they can be seen simply as reports of what has occurred. It is easiest for descriptions to be nonevaluative since, by definition, they need not judge but only describe. However, the same can be true of quantifications and labels. Although people generally have judgments they associate with certain quantifications and labels, they need not be evaluative per se.

For example, if a student earns a 75 on a test because he or she got three answers correct and one incorrect, that simply indicates what has occurred. Depending on the nature of the test, three out of four may be excellent, good, average, or poor. Certainly we have come to associate 75 with average because it often equates to a C, but this is only a common perception and need not be the case.

Perhaps the test was meant to be so challenging that getting even one question correct is an excellent performance. Symbols may seem more naturally evaluative, especially given the pervasive A through F paradigm, but it is possible to imagine labels that are linked to nonevaluative descriptors. Thus, one need not necessarily view a label or a number as an evaluation. Truly evaluative grades must have an explicit narrative judgment to which they are at least linked.

In the end, defining a grade as an evaluation simply means one is doing more than reporting what has occurred—one is placing a judgment on the student's work. Thus, evaluative grades must include, or at least be linked to, words or phrases (e.g., excellent, good, average, poor) that make a qualitative judgment.

The final way of describing a grade is as a ranking, which is only slightly different than an evaluation. A ranking is a form of evaluation that evaluates work relative to some other work. What it is relative to is the third part of our generic definition of a grade, and options for this are dealt with later in this chapter. Suffice it to say that in order to rank work, it seems necessary to use a number or symbol so that ranking can be more easily determined.

The Topic of the Information

The topic of the information is even more complicated than the type of information. Broadly speaking, this category has two elements: the *what* and the *when*. *What* can refer to a student's skill level, performance, or progress. *When* indicates the period of time over which, or moment in time at which, *what* is measured. In the case of a grade on an individual assessment, *when* clearly refers to the time period at which the assessment was completed, but when it comes to summative grades for either a unit of study, a term, or a school year, one must be more deliberate in specifying the *when*.

Let us first define the *whats*. Student learning refers to how well a student has mastered the curriculum—the particular material that the teacher intends her or him to learn. On the other hand, while it need not necessarily be so, student skill level could refer to attributes and abilities that are not a part of the curriculum taught by the teacher. For example, in a unit on solving algebraic equations, a measurement of student learning would entail to what degree the student learned how to solve these equations; however, a measurement of skill level might take into account speed and efficiency, two abilities not necessarily needed to show that one has learned something. Further, student skill level might take into account a student's ability to solve problems above and beyond what is a part of the curriculum.

Next we must distinguish student learning and skill level from student performance. A student who has learned a great deal and has a high skill level could very easily perform poorly on an assessment due to lack of effort or any number of other factors that could lead to a performance that does not reflect his or her learning or skill level. Imagine a student who skips class every day that there is a test and never makes them up. On all other days he is diligent, attentive, does his homework, and prepares for the assessments, but just doesn't take them. His performance would be quite poor, but that would say nothing about what he learned and what his skill level is.

The final option for *what* is being reported is student progress. This could refer to a measurement of learning, skill level, or performance, but it would measure these factors against a student's starting point as opposed to an objective standard or set of criteria. This envisions a scenario in which "higher" grades could go to students whose skill level may be lower because they have come further over the period of time being measured.

While it is absolutely necessary to stipulate a time period if one is reporting a student's progress, it is also necessary for the other *whats* as well. A grade can indicate the level of a student's learning or skills at a given time, or it can attempt to approximate some aggregate over a period of time. A grade can similarly report aggregate performance or performance on one particular occasion.

All grades measured over a period of time are, by nature, summative grades, but the different options have far-reaching implications. Let us use skill level as an example. If grades reflect an average over time, then one could end up with two students with the exact same skill level at the end of a term having very different summative grades because they may have started at different levels. On the other hand, if one chooses to give a summative grade that reflects where students are at the end of the term, then these two students would earn the same grade (for a more detailed discussion, see chapter 5).

Keep in mind that if one is attempting to report progress, then the student with the lower summative grade when averaged would actually be more deserving of a higher grade than the student with equal skill level who did not come as far over the course of the term.

This all presupposes that we need to give summative grades, an assumption that educators may wish to question.

Context for the Information

Finally, we come to the third part of what grades may represent, the context for the information provided by a grade. One need not add this part of the definition if one is reporting on progress, since that report is by definition relative to where a student began. However, when grades symbolize or describe without providing a context, they become less meaningful; they become almost meaningless when evaluating or ranking without context.

Suppose an A is given the descriptor *excellent*. We must still ask, what does *excellent* mean? Does it mean one of the best in a particular group of students—a class, a school, a grade or age level statewide or even nationally? Or does *excellent* mean a student has done something or displayed skills that met a certain defined standard of excellence? Of course a grade could mean *excellent* in some absolute sense, relative to all other possible outcomes. As one can clearly see, a grade means something very different depending on what it is relative to. These options speak for themselves and thus do not need careful scrutiny, but it should be clear why this element of the definition of grades is so critical.

THE IMPORTANCE OF TRANSPARENCY

It is worth going to these lengths to show both how complicated the very concept of a grade is, and that to use the term *grade* without defining what it represents provides very little information. Consider the following: "I got a B." "My average is 76." "My project was unsatisfactory." While we may have a general sense of what those things mean, carefully considering how many different ways in which the term *grade* can be defined, we realize that those statements actually give us very little specific or useful information. Thus, if grades are to provide students with feedback on their work that can lead to further learning, teachers and schools must clearly define what their grades represent.

Further chapters examine the positives and negatives of the various options defined in this chapter, but the real point is that it may matter less what teachers and schools decide they want their grades to reflect than that they are transparent in defining them. If students and their parents are to use the information in a way that is supportive of learning, then they must be made perfectly aware of what the grades they are receiving mean. Teachers and schools should also keep in mind that they do not need to limit themselves to using only one type of grade, and certainly may use a range of them, so long as they are clear about what each grade reflects.

While transparency may be of foremost importance, it does matter which type of grade one chooses, and deciding this depends on why you are using grades to begin with. As stated earlier, grades are used by colleges and employers to sort and select students, but that should not be our purpose in using them within schools. Our purpose should be to support and enhance student learning. Thus, in order to help us decide what type of grades to assign, we must now look carefully at the purposes for which grades can be used and the effects that each purpose may have on student learning.

Chapter 2

The Pedagogical Purposes of Grades

SUPERFICIAL VERSUS UNDERLYING PURPOSES

Chapter 1 suggested many possible ways in which grades can be defined, with each different definition leading to significant distinctions in what a grade is attempting to report. Depending on which definition is selected, grades can serve many different purposes. If transparency is of utmost importance when defining grades, of equal importance are the purposes for which grades are used. One might argue that each of the possible definitions suggested in chapter 1 can be viewed as an explanation of the purpose of the grade (e.g., to quantify a student's performance, to describe a student's skills), but these are superficial purposes and refer to the function that the grades serve, not a school's or a teacher's underlying purpose—their *pedagogical* purpose—for giving grades. Grades may rank student achievement or they may symbolize a student's progress, but still we must ask why we want to do these things in the first place: why are we giving grades?

As suggested in the introduction, grading is important because it has the potential to do three things:

1. To provide data about students upon which to base decisions
2. To motivate students
3. To provide students with feedback on their work

This chapter takes a close look at the legitimacy and implications of each of these three potential purposes for the use of grades.

GRADES AS DATA UPON WHICH TO BASE DECISIONS

The data generated by grades can be used for internal or external purposes. The most obvious of the external purposes for which this data can be used is to rank or sort students in order to assist colleges and employers in making decisions about them. As stated in the introduction, this is not a pedagogically legitimate purpose for schools to consider since it is not related to student learning and, as we will see, may in fact have a detrimental effect on that learning.

This is not to say that there is anything wrong with the sharing of grades with these constituencies, but it should not play a role in the process of determining how to grade students. Admissions officers and employers can use whatever grades are provided to help them do the sorting, but producing grades that are user-friendly for these two groups should not be a concern of educators. Admissions officers and employers may be dismayed at the prospect of having to do more work in sorting students, but in the end, they will be happier if they are getting better-educated applicants due to more pedagogically sound grading policies.

While currently there is justifiable controversy over the legitimacy of standardized tests such as the Scholastic Aptitude Test (SAT), one of the central purposes of the SAT is to help colleges sort out students due to the fact that trying to compare grades from different schools across the country amounted to a futile exercise in comparing apples to oranges.[1] Perhaps the solution for admissions offices is, in fact, less reliance on grades and more emphasis on better standardized measurements.

The other way in which the data provided by grades can be used externally is when reported to governments—local, state, and even federal—for the purpose of making decisions about educational policy. This reporting could potentially provide important data with which policymakers could make decisions that would positively affect student learning, making it a legitimate use of grades, but one that remains outside the scope of this book, particularly since this data need not come in the form of individual student grades and, in this case, need not even be reported to students or parents.

Internally, data can also be used to rank or sort students and to help make decisions about curriculum and pedagogy. Let's start with the internal ranking and sorting of students. Schools may use grades to rank or sort their students for purposes such as the recognition and celebration of excellence or the tracking of students. Recognition or celebration of excellence (honor rolls, dean's lists, etc.) may simply represent particular methods of motivating students and giving them feedback. If such pedagogical considerations are not the reasons for these practices, then they are doing no more than generating data for external constituencies such as colleges and employers, and thus they cease to serve the purpose of supporting student learning.

Grades can also be used internally to rank and sort students for the purpose of tracking them into different courses, which may be a more legitimate purpose for grades since it represents an internal use of the data generated by grades for a pedagogical purpose. Still, there remains a great deal of controversy surrounding tracking and its effects on student learning, but suffice it to say that, if deemed pedagogically sound, it remains a possible justification for using grades to rank or sort students internally.

A less controversial use of grades to generate data internally is to do so for the purpose of informing future practice. In fact, it is almost axiomatic in the field of education today that data should be used in this manner. For example, a large number of students earning grades that indicate a deficiency in a certain skill is a clear reason for changing the method of instruction. That said, data of this sort does not need to be in the form of a traditional grade and need not even be reported to anyone beyond the teacher. If this is the case, one might even hesitate to refer to such data as grades, looking at the data as a formative assessment of sorts—one that is not intended to be graded in the traditional sense of the term.

In sum, there are a number of ways to use the data generated by grades, but educators should only be concerned with generating data if it plays a genuine role in supporting and enhancing student learning.

GRADES AS MOTIVATORS

We most commonly think of grades as rewards and punishments—the carrot and stick in the model of the psychological behaviorists. The argument here is simple: grades are useful because they motivate students to learn by rewarding them for learning with good grades and punishing them for not learning with bad grades. On its face and without deeper examination, this seems to make sense and, further, may even suggest that grades are not only beneficent, but necessary. After all, one might argue, if teachers didn't give grades, students would not do their work and hence would learn very little.

However, motivation and its relationship to human behavior may not be quite as simple as some behaviorists suggest. Let's examine the argument more closely:

> Grades are useful because they motivate students to learn by rewarding them for learning with good grades and punishing them for not learning with bad grades.

The first thing to consider is that it is unclear to what concept of grade this argument refers, and chapter 1 showed that a grade can be many things and that each has very different implications. Most likely, this argument assumes a traditional view in which grades are symbols of student performance. Students would compare their symbols to those of other students in the hopes of having the best symbols, with the further assumption that having the best symbols would lead to some further reward (e.g., a college acceptance letter or a good job). Now, if one thinks of grades as a description of student learning, then the idea of a grade even being a reward or a punishment is brought into question since a description of what has occurred cannot, by definition, be either a reward or a punishment.

The second part of this argument that raises some questions is the very idea that grades motivate students to learn, when in actuality they may motivate a different behavior. Rather than motivating learning, grades may simply motivate students to complete their work, and while this may lead to learning, it is not the same thing. Doing one's work does not guarantee that deep and lasting learning will occur.

A perhaps even more radical notion is that grades actually inhibit learning. In order to explore this idea, a good place to start is Daniel Pink's 2009 book *Drive: The Surprising Truth about What Motivates Us*, which details over seventy years of research into human motivation, leading to some startling and far-reaching conclusions. Pink's book starts in 1949 when psychology professor Harry Harlow, observing some lab monkeys, made a startling discovery: "unbidden by any outside urging and unprompted by the experimenters the monkeys began playing with puzzles with focus, determination, and what looked like enjoyment."[2] Pink explains that up until then scientists had been aware of two drives for human behavior: the internal biological drive—eating, reproducing, and so on—and the external drive—rewards and punishments.[3]

The behavior of these monkeys was motivated by neither of these, which suggested a third drive, some form of intrinsic motivation. Assuming that this drive was subordinate to the others, Harlow rewarded the monkeys with raisins in an attempt to enhance their puzzle solving, but it had the exact opposite effect. Pink tells us, "the monkeys actually made *more* errors and solved the puzzles *less* frequently" when the rewards were introduced.[4] Thus, Harlow was led to conclude that "introduction of food in the present experiment served to disrupt performance."[5] Far from motivating better work, rewards actually led to poorer performance.

This startlingly counterintuitive finding was not explained until Harlow's work was picked up by Edward Deci in 1969. Deci's experiments not only confirmed the existence of this intrinsic motivation, they actually suggested that it is stronger over the long term than the motivation of punishments and rewards. Further—and here is the explanation for why Harlow's monkeys performed more poorly when given food as a reward for solving puzzles— Deci's experiments showed that punishments and rewards diminish intrinsic motivation.[6]

Deci's experiment looked at two groups of people solving puzzles over a three-day period. On day 1, neither group was paid, and naturally their effort and engagement level was the same. On day 2, Group A was paid for their work, and, not surprisingly, they worked harder and longer on the puzzles than Group B. On the third day, Deci told Group A he could no longer pay them for their work. Here is Pink's description of the results:

> the subjects in the never-been-paid Group B actually played with the puzzle for a little longer than they had in the previous sessions. Maybe they were becoming even more engaged; maybe it was just a statistical quirk. But the subjects in Group A, who previously had been paid, responded differently. They now spent significantly *less* time playing with the puzzle—not only about two minutes less than during their paid session, but about a full minute less than in their first session when they initially encountered, and obviously enjoyed, the puzzles. [7]

Deci confirmed these findings in two additional studies, concluding, "when money is used as an external reward for some activity, the subjects lose intrinsic interest for the activity."[8] Thus, in Pink's words, "Rewards can deliver a short-term boost—just as a jolt of caffeine can keep you cranking for a few more hours. But the effect wears off—and worse, can reduce a person's longer-term motivation to continue a project."[9]

How do these findings relate to grades? Given that intrinsic motivation seems to be the strongest drive over a sustained period of time, it is natural that one of the goals of education should be to generate intrinsic motivation to learn. Does this mean that grades are like the monetary rewards in Deci's experiments—they provide short-term motivation, but diminish it in the long term? If this is the case, then grades would be poor motivators for the behavior that educators genuinely wish to see from their students. Let us examine the analogy more carefully to see if it fits.

First, although students are not all the same and people are not all motivated in the same way, it must be acknowledged that grades do motivate large numbers of students. Yet during this process, the question remains whether or not students learn as deeply when the learning process is a means to an end—the reward/grade—as opposed to being an end in and of itself. Furthermore, we must look down the road and wonder if it is detrimental to motivate students with grades because school will one day end, and, just like the day Deci stopped paying his subjects, their work ethic, engagement, and consequently their performance may decline.

Deci even mentions students directly, writing, "one who is interested in developing and enhancing intrinsic motivation in children, employees, students, etc., should not concentrate on external control systems such as monetary rewards."[10] Are good grades the same thing as money—a reward for good work—or are they simply a record of the good work? This depends on the nature of the grade and how it is used. As stated previously, when grades are descriptions, they are clearly not meant to be rewards—yet that may not stop students from viewing them as such since they can compare their descriptors to those given to other students, and the descriptive grades may still be used in determining outcomes such as college acceptances. Furthermore, when grades are used deliberately for the purpose of ranking and recognition, then clearly they can be seen as rewards, making it even more likely that learning will be viewed as no more than a means to an end, subsequently diminishing any intrinsic motivation to learn—motivation that will encourage students to learn more deeply and to continue learning even after the test has been given.

Thus, it seems that in whatever grading system teachers or schools choose, they must do whatever is possible to diminish the focus on grades and shift that focus to the actual learning. This is a difficult shift to make in a society in which people think that grades are a high-stakes game, even all the way down to elementary school. Imagine the parents of a third-grade student losing sleep over whether or not their child's grades will get him placed in the accelerated math program, believing that his academic future will largely be determined by this decision. This otherwise ridiculous notion gains credence with the argument that getting on the accelerated track early is the only way a student can get through AP Calculus by high school graduation, and this is what he needs if he wants to go to Harvard, and if he wants to be successful in life he has to go to Harvard (or at least some place like it). Attitudes like this put the focus squarely on the result, leaving little time to think about the learning process. Of course, the irony is that deep learning is what really leads to success (not to mention happiness) in life.

But with the perception that the stakes are extremely high, it is easy to see the challenge of shifting the focus from grades to learning. This is exactly why theorists such as Alfie Kohn believe that we must end grading in education. Kohn argues that there are three main effects of grading:

1. Grades tend to reduce a student's interest in the learning itself.
2. Grades tend to reduce a student's preference for challenging tasks.
3. Grades tend to reduce the quality of student thinking.

Kohn further suggests the following five reasons educators should eliminate grades:

1. Grades aren't valid, reliable, or objective.
2. Grades distort the curriculum.
3. Grades waste a lot of time that could be spent on learning.
4. Grades encourage cheating.
5. Grades spoil teachers' relationships with students. [11]

Kohn's argument is fairly convincing in theory, but in practice, it is unlikely that grades will go away anytime soon. This is mainly because of two things: (1) our society's powerful desire to sort and rank students, and (2) the ever-present challenge of making fundamental changes within educational institutions. However, these obstacles do not necessarily inhibit us from ensuring that our grades are more than simply rewards and punishments, and from actively working to de-emphasize grades in order to put the focus on learning.

Yet we must also consider the other side of the story, which suggests that perhaps Kohn is too quick to write off grades, for the following three reasons:

1. While grades may diminish intrinsic motivation, they still work as motivators and are needed as such in certain cases.
2. They can be used to help educators inform future practice.
3. They can become powerful tools for providing students with feedback.

Therefore, let us look at when and how they can be used effectively. Daniel Pink's argument in *Drive* is focused mainly on work that has potential to motivate us intrinsically, but instead fails to provide the motivation because of the implementation of a system of punishments and rewards. However, we must acknowledge that not all work has the potential to motivate us intrinsically. Students are not interested in all classes, and some important information and concepts can, in fact, be boring.

Hence, students may need the initial motivation provided by grades to get them to put in the time and effort in a less intrinsically interesting yet nonetheless critical topic. This will help them to attain and develop important knowledge and skills that will allow them to access and understand more advanced and innately interesting levels of a subject that may then generate intrinsic motivation. One thinks of the grunt work of memorizing multiplication tables or monotonous drills to improve reading skills that, while not intrinsically motivating, will one day allow a student to study high-level mathematics and read *The Great Gatsby*—two things that will be tremendously interesting for those properly prepared to take on these challenges.

Another common scenario with adolescents is one in which a student does not know that he or she will find something interesting unless he or she first does some work to learn about it. In this case, grades can be very helpful in providing the initial motivation for what begins as work but might quickly become a passion. One can imagine a passionate expert in some field of study admitting that if she had not had grades hanging over her head in high school, she never would have studied hard. If she hadn't made that extra effort, which at the time was done to get a good grade, she never would have realized how interesting her given field of study is.

Thus, we see that grades are able to provide important motivation for students, especially early in one's academic career. Still, one must remain aware that grades can be dangerous if they become the sole focus of a student's education. Hence, as educators, we must work to devise a system of grading that provides the appropriate amount of initial motivation without diminishing the intrinsic motivation developed through the joy of learning. Most likely this will be a system of grades that is much more about describing student learning relative to a standard than one that labels student learning for the purpose of ranking or sorting students—a practice that will all too often function more as a system of rewards and punishments than a motivation to learn deeply. Further, the hope is that teachers, regardless of what system of grading they are required to use in their classes, can, through addressing the issue frequently, shift the focus of their classes from grades to learning.

GRADES AS PROVIDERS OF FEEDBACK

The third pedagogical purpose for which grades can be used is to provide feedback for students. Feedback on one's work is critical to making improvement, and thus, it is essential that grades provide the feedback necessary to bring about improvement in student learning. Returning to the intricacies of the definition of *grade*, it is first important to consider what a teacher is using a grade to give feedback on. Here the distinction between grades on individual assessments and grades that are summative and appear on a report card is critical. If the grade is on an individual assessment, then clearly the feedback should reflect one or both of the following:

- A student's performance on that individual assessment task
- A student's progress since performances on previous assessments

A summative grade has potential to provide feedback on many more things:

- A student's learning
- A student's skill level at a certain time
- A student's average skill level over a period of time
- A student's average performance on a number of assessment tasks
- A student's progress over a certain period of time

These are all important things for students to get feedback upon, and the most pedagogically sound grading systems try to accomplish all of them in one way or another. Clearly, the form the grades take will make a big difference in determining whether or not they can be effective in providing this feedback.

First, consider the three criteria necessary for feedback to be effective:

1. It must be relevant to the learning goals.
2. It must be detailed and specific.
3. It must be useful for improvement.

Quantifications, symbols, and rankings seem ill-suited to fit these criteria. Thus, someone who truly wishes to use grades to provide feedback for students will be more likely to use narrative descriptions or evaluations.

Additionally, it seems more important to provide feedback through grades on individual assessments than to do so with grades that are summative. This is exactly the rationale behind the use of formative assessments, which are assessments *for*, not *of*, learning, and consequently are not meant to be used as part of the summative grade.[12] Whether or not a teacher deems an assessment as formative, he or she may wish to consider grades of the descriptive nature on all individual assessments, even if the final summative grade is a quantification or symbol.

Furthermore, if one is required to quantify performances on individual assessments or the assessment is one that lends itself to easy quantification (e.g., a multiple choice test) it is important to accompany this with some narrative description that can provide feedback that meets the above criteria. This means that, even on the "simplest" of tests, teachers need to do more than mark right and wrong; they need to look carefully and attempt to intuit what a student's answers reveal about his or her knowledge and skills, and then provide some feedback that is relevant, specific, and useful.

Teachers are justified in responding to this suggestion by pointing out that, given large class sizes and other obligations, they do not have the time to give such specific feedback. It is idealistic, but this book is trying to lay out the ideal scenario, and those school systems and administrators who wish to maximize the ability of their grading systems to support student learning and have the means to do so will make sure that teachers have the time to grade in this manner. In a less ideal world, where time is limited for every teacher, the traditional "see me" at the top of a student's work can be effective since it saves time, and those students willing to make the effort to see you will be the ones who benefit from more specific feedback.

Based on the above, one can be certain that theorists such as Alfie Kohn will argue that feedback is critical but there is absolutely no need for it to come in the form of a grade. However, the argument here simply expands the definition of grade to include the feedback given, and while Kohn and those who share his viewpoint may suggest that feedback and grades are two different things, the hope is that in fusing the two, educators will move toward grading systems that Kohn would find much more pedagogically sound—ones that enhance rather than take away from student learning.

Even if a school is not able to divorce itself from a system of grades that provides user-friendly data for colleges and employers, it need only do this with summative grades, and can at the same time make sure that grades on individual assessments are aimed at giving feedback to students. Descriptive grades and even evaluative grades that are narrative in form are more likely to provide students with the feedback they need, but not when accompanied by a corresponding symbol or quantification because students will focus on the latter and not on the feedback. Thus, teachers may wish to conceal the quantification or symbol (if one is necessary) from the students, forcing them to focus only on the feedback given. [13]

Such a practice will help shift the focus of the students from the summative grade to the process of learning itself. The irony here is that students (and their parents) may feel lost without a quantification or a symbol—no matter how much feedback a teacher gives. They will likely say, "I have no idea how I am doing." This concern is a clear indication that the student or parents are not looking carefully at the feedback and are more concerned with grades than learning. This alerts the teacher that it's time to have a conversation with this student and his or her parents—a conversation that hopefully will begin to change their mindsets and one that would never have taken place if the teacher had continued to give them the quantification or symbol that they so desperately wanted to see.

The work of psychologist Carol Dweck is extremely relevant to any consideration of how grades provide feedback. In her groundbreaking work *Mindset: The New Psychology of Success*, Dweck outlines the critical difference between having a "fixed mindset"—one that "believes your qualities are carved in stone"—and a "growth mindset"—one that "is based on the belief that your basic qualities are things that you can cultivate through your efforts." [14] With a fixed mindset, individuals believe that they either have certain talents or they do not. In either case, this will preclude them from growing since they don't even believe growth is a possibility. On the other hand, with a growth mindset, one's belief that one can grow and develop opens up these very possibilities.

Clearly, educators should work to help their students develop growth mindsets, and Dweck's theory makes it clear that a student's mindset will be affected by the type of feedback that he or she is given. Dweck writes of parents and teachers: "their judgments, their lessons, their motivating techniques often send the wrong message." [15] Dweck elaborates on the feedback that we give students: "Every word and action can send a message. It tells children—or students, or athletes—how to think about themselves. It can be a fixed-mindset message that says: *You have permanent traits and I'm judging them.* Or it can be a growth-mindset message that says: *You are a developing person and I am interested in your development.*" [16] This means that in the feedback they give to students, teachers must be certain to focus on process rather than results and on the effort and strategies employed rather than talent. When students have success, the feedback must make it clear to them that the success was the result of hard work and effective strategies, rather than some innate intelligence that they may or may not possess. When they fail, students must see the failure not as a judgment upon them, but rather on the work they produced in a given instant—work that can certainly improve with a greater effort and perhaps a different approach.

What this suggests is that certain types of grades may do a better job promoting a growth mindset than others. Certainly quantifications or symbols are more likely to suggest a fixed mindset since they are labels with which students may begin to personally identify. It is much easier for students to permanently label themselves "B students" than it would be to define themselves based on a grade that was a narrative evaluation or one meant only to describe their learning and/or performance.

Symbols can also contribute to the development of a fixed mindset because of the lack of nuanced and specific information they provide. Imagine the student who earns Bs year after year and thinks, "I just can't seem to improve as a student. I never make any gains in my learning, so I guess I will always be average." No gains in learning? That couldn't be further from the truth. What this string of Bs fails to make clear to the student is that the course of study has grown increasingly complicated and challenging. Thus, a string of identical grades actually represents tremendous growth in learning. Maintaining a certain letter grade level over a period of time, despite the fact that the label remains the same, actually represents growth.

Similarly, rankings can also contribute to a fixed mindset. Even if a student is making progress, if other students to which that student is compared are making progress as well, then there will be little change to that student's rank, encouraging the belief that intelligence is fixed.

It also seems clear that reporting on a student's progress or skill level at a certain period of time is more likely to encourage a growth mindset than grades that report an average performance or skill level over a period of time. In some ways, averages make it difficult to represent the true extent of student growth. As an extreme example, a student who begins a year doing work that earns Fs and then finishes the year doing work that earns As gets a C for the year—the same grade as someone who did C-level work all along. In such a system, the lack of clarity regarding the reporting of student progress can make it difficult for a student to develop a growth mindset.

In sum, for a grade to give feedback that will help a student develop a growth mindset, it must either provide evidence of student growth or suggest the possibility of growth. Ideally, this grade, whether "good" or "bad," will make it clear that it is a representation of a certain level of effort and particular strategies as opposed to a measure of innate ability. Even if a teacher is required to give a grade that may encourage a fixed mindset, he or she can make certain to accompany that grade with comments that are growth oriented.

WHY GIVE GRADES?

This careful examination of the pedagogical purpose for grades should have made it clear that there are very good reasons to give grades, reasons that can help to support and enhance student learning. These reasons are to generate data with which decisions can be made about future practice, to motivate students, and to provide them with feedback.

The best grading systems will accomplish all three of these purposes, but one must be ever vigilant in their use, for, as suggested, grades can also work against the very purposes for which they were designed. More specifically, grades can take away from long-term motivation, and they can provide damaging feedback. This is particularly the case when the stakes are too high, when grades, rather than learning, become the focus for students and their parents, and when they encourage a fixed mindset. This all points to a need for the de-emphasis of grades, for it is through this very de-emphasis that they can become effective as tools to enhance learning, helping to raise the overall achievement of our nation's students.

NOTES

1. Nicholas Lemann, *The Big Test: The Secret History of the American Meritocracy* (New York: Farrar, Straus and Giroux, 2000), 96.

2. Daniel Pink, *Drive: The Surprising Truth about What Motivates Us* (New York: Riverhead Books, 2009), 2.

3. Ibid., 2–3.

4. Ibid., 3–4.

5. Harry F. Harlow, Margaret Kuenne Harlow, and Donald R. Meyer, "Learning Motivated by a Manipulative Drive," *Journal of Experimental Psychology* 40.2 (1950): 232, quoted in Pink, *Drive*, 3.

6. Pink, *Drive*, 5–9.

7. Ibid., 7–8.

8. Edward L. Deci, "Effects of Externally Mediated Rewards on Intrinsic Motivation," *Journal of Personality and Social Psychology* 18 (1971): 114, quoted in Pink, *Drive*, 8.

9. Pink, *Drive*, 8.

10. Edward L. Deci, "Intrinsic Motivation, External Reinforcement, and Inequity," *Journal of Personality and Social Psychology* 22 (1972): 119-120, quoted in Pink, *Drive*, 8.

11. Alfie Kohn, "From Degrading to De-grading," *High School Magazine* (March 1999), http://www.alfiekohn.org/teaching/fdtd-g.htm.

12. Richard Stiggins, "Assessment Crisis: The Absence of Assessment for Learning," *Phi Delta Kappan* 83.10 (2002): 761. Here Stiggins explains that while formative assessment and assessment for learning are not the same thing, formative assessment is certainly a part of assessment for learning.

13. For a more detailed discussion of this topic, see Timothy Quinn, "A Crash Course on Giving Grades," *Phi Delta Kappan* 93.4 (2011): 57–59.

14. Carol Dweck, *Mindset: The New Psychology of Success* (New York: Ballantine, 2006), 6–7.

15. Ibid., 173.

16. Ibid.

Part 2

Issues in Grading

Part 1 of this book looked at the concepts of grades and grading from a theoretical perspective—examining what they are and for what purposes they can (and should) be used. With that theoretical underpinning, the book now moves to an examination of important practical issues related to grades and grading. Hopefully, what has been established in part 1 will help clarify the issues addressed in part 2 and will help teachers and administrators to better solve these important and often controversial problems.

Chapter 3

Grade Inflation

CONCERNS WITH GRADE INFLATION

Grade inflation is one of the most common grading-related issues discussed in schools today, particularly at the high school and college levels. Many teachers and administrators are concerned with this phenomenon, but educators are not the only ones worried about it. It is often taken up by social critics and op-ed writers across the country who cite the trend of rising grades as evidence of decreased rigor and lower academic standards, all of which, they postulate, contribute to a decline in the strength of students produced by American schools.

Thanks to the coddling of grade inflation, critics argue, students lack the grit and resilience—not to mention skills—necessary for success in today's world. Two of the most prominent critics of grade inflation are Stuart Rojstaczer and Christopher Healy. Rojstaczer and Healy have spent a great deal of time analyzing grades at the college level and postulate that higher grades—which they refer to as "grade inflation"—will result in decreased motivation and hence, less learning.[1] Critics also complain that rising grades make it difficult to differentiate among students. Emory University professor Mark Bauerlein writes in the *New York Daily News*, "When employers can't depend on colleges to single out the best and brightest, higher education has failed its most fundamental duty."[2]

Although educators must take these criticisms seriously, it is worth pointing out some potential flaws in their arguments. While Rojstaczer and Healy have provided clear data showing that grades are, in fact, rising, they can only speculate on the causes. They come to the conclusion that standards have been lowered, assuming that the quality of work cannot have gone up. While there is evidence that students spend fewer hours on homework than in the past,[3] data that proves that the actual quality of work has gone down is hard to come by. As for Bauerlein's argument that singling out "the best and brightest" is higher education's "most fundamental duty," this book argues that the most fundamental duty of education at every level is to help students learn.

Less likely to take issue with grade inflation are students and parents, who are generally pleased to see higher grades. However, even they sometimes object to grade inflation since they believe it belittles the performance of those (generally referring to themselves or their own children) who *really* earned and deserve the high grades.

HIGHER ACHIEVEMENT OR LOWER STANDARDS?

This book deliberately refers to grade inflation as an issue or a phenomenon, not as a problem, because whether or not rising grades are a problem is exactly what must be determined before deciding how the situation should be handled. In fact, one should first ask whether or not grade inflation actually exists. There seems to be little doubt that grades are getting higher. Yet those who claim that grades are "inflated" use the term pejoratively to imply that there is something artificial about these higher grades—that the performance they are meant to label is somewhat inferior to what the grade represents. If this were true, then that certainly would be a problem, since by no means should students be assigned higher grades than they deserve. However, we must determine whether grades are being inflated or whether student performance is simply improving.

Answering the previous question requires a great deal of challenging and complicated research. In the end, it is unlikely that this research would provide an objective answer since so much of it would be based on subjective judgment. This is particularly so at the higher levels of academia, where grading often refers to the assessment of abstract thinking skills, not just right or wrong answers. Undoubtedly, in some cases, rising grades may be the result of inflation due to the pressure on teachers in a student-as-consumer paradigm, along with a host of other factors, including an emphasis on self-esteem at the lower levels of schooling and the high stakes associated with grades at the upper levels of schooling.

Still, we must consider the number of factors that might suggest improved student performance as the cause of higher grades. Among these are improved teaching, greater effort and effectiveness on the part of students, a general increase in human intelligence and skills, and increased access to educational opportunities. Most notably, the work of James Flynn offers evidence that human beings have displayed an increase in certain intellectual skills over recent history.[4] Thus, rising grades might not be the result of artificial inflation, but simply of human progress.

The issue of grade inflation is also complicated by the inevitable lack of consistency, and the reluctance to carefully and precisely define standards of achievement. Chapter 1 spoke to the importance of having a general definition of a grade, but it is also important that schools define particular grades within the grading system. In response to the complaints of too many As, one might ask what an A even means.

Here is an interesting example that illustrates both the lack of clarity regarding whether or not higher grades are even a problem and the difficulty of discussing the issue without precise definitions for grades. A 2005 *New York Times* article titled "Students Receive Fewer A's and Princeton Calls It Progress" explains Princeton's attempt to tackle grade inflation and how the school was pleased when they were able to reduce the number of As given to students.[5] Yet never once does the article define what an A is—one only hopes that Princeton did so, but a useful definition seems unlikely. They may have defined an A as "exceptional work," which is rather vague and also causes one to ask, why wouldn't teachers and administrators want more students doing exceptional work?

It is also interesting to note that the article refers consistently to the "giving" of grades. Most teachers will be quick to explain that grades are earned rather than given. If this is the case, how could a teacher lower the quantity of As earned, since the grades are determined by the work of the students? More importantly, if teachers wish for their students to succeed, why would they possibly want fewer students to earn As?

FAULTY UNDERLYING BELIEFS ABOUT THE NATURE OF INTELLIGENCE

Is the problem really about standards getting lower, or is it about too many As? Many would say that those are one and the same thing: that if you raise standards, fewer students will earn As. Yet one is forced to wonder about the underlying reasons why people are uncomfortable with lots of students earning As. The answer is a faulty belief about the nature of intelligence. At the heart of complaints about grade inflation is a belief that only certain people are capable of achieving at the highest levels, that there is some innate element of academic ability that not all people have access to. For a long time, such an argument may have seemed plausible, but in recent years, evidence has mounted that intelligence is not a fixed attribute entirely determined by genetics.

In his 2010 book *The Genius in All of Us*, David Shenk takes his reader through a great deal of research that argues, "While it would be folly to suggest that anyone can literally do or become anything . . . the new science tells us that it's equally foolish to think that mediocrity is built into most of us."[6] Shenk goes on: "Our abilities are not set in genetic stone. They are soft and sculptable, far into adulthood. With humility, with hope, and with extraordinary determination, greatness is something to which any kid—of any age—can aspire."[7]

Chapter 2 of Shenk's book, "Intelligence Is a Process, Not a Thing," explores an idea postulated by Alfred Binet, the inventor of the original IQ test. Binet writes in his *Modern Ideas about Children*, "[Some] assert that an individual's intelligence is a fixed quantity which cannot be increased. We must protest and react against this brutal pessimism."[8] Binet goes on to assert that "with practice, training, and above all method, we manage to increase our attention, our memory, our judgment, and literally to become more intelligent than we were before."[9] In contrast, Lewis Terman adapted Binet's theories to create the more modern form of the IQ test, a test that purports to measure a person's "native intelligence." With its perfect bell curve distribution, Shenk explains, Terman's test sends the message to those who take it: "your intelligence is something you were given, not something you earned."[10]

Shenk then dispels the belief promoted by Terman's IQ test, relying heavily on the work of psychologist Robert Sternberg. Sternberg's work led him to conclude that a new theory of intelligence was needed. He concluded that rather than an innate or fixed trait, "intelligence represents a set of competencies in development."[11] Later in the same essay, Sternberg writes, "abilities as developing forms of expertise [result from] interaction with the demands of the environment."[12] That is a more complicated way of stating that certain environmental factors—like, say, a demanding school or an engaging teacher—can result in enhanced ability in all students. This is not to say that genetics play no role in achievement whatsoever; in fact, the main argument of Shenk's book is that intelligence is a result of the interaction between genes and environment and that because of the role the environment plays, no matter what the content of our genes, our abilities are not fixed. Thus, we should not assume that only a select few are capable of high achievement.

This research into human intelligence changes the framework of the debate over grade inflation. If one believes that all students are capable of high achievement, then more high achievement is a positive thing. Good teachers try to help each of their students achieve highly and are proud and pleased whenever any individual student is able to make significant improvement. Thus, it is contradictory that teachers would find it a problem when this happens for a larger number of students. A desire for a bell curve in grade distribution sends the wrong message to students about achievement—a message that, according to Carol Dweck, can be very harmful and that itself can perpetuate lower achievement.[13]

THE PROBLEM WITH BELL CURVES

It is worth examining the concept of the bell curve more thoroughly, since opponents of rising grades often suggest that this is what grade distribution should look like for any given group of students—a few high achievers, a lot in the middle, and a few low achievers. In his article "Five Obstacles to Grading Reform," Thomas R. Guskey cites the belief that "grade distribution should resemble a bell curve" as obstacle number two to the ability of grading policies to progress along with other elements of education. [14]

Guskey explains that the following is a flawed belief: "if scores on intelligence tests tend to resemble a bell-shaped curve—and intelligence is clearly related to achievement—then grade distribution should be similar." [15] Addressing this notion, Guskey quickly points out that bell-shaped curves describe "the distribution of randomly occurring events *when nothing intervenes*." [16] Because teaching is an intervention that should affect student achievement, the argument for a bell curve falls apart. It is worth quoting, at length, the poignant analogy that he provides:

> If we conducted an experiment on crop yield in agriculture, for example, we would expect the results to resemble a normal curve. A few fertile fields would produce a high yield; a few infertile fields would produce a low yield; and most would produce an average yield, clustering around the center of the distribution.
>
> But if we intervene in that process—say we add a fertilizer—we would hope to attain a very different distribution of results. Specifically, we would hope to have all fields, or nearly all, produce a high yield. The ideal result would be for all fields to move to the high end of the distribution. In fact, if the distribution of crop yield after our intervention still resembled a normal bell-shaped curve, that would show that our intervention had failed because it made no difference. [17]

Thus, based on Guskey's reasoning, a bell-curve distribution of grades reflects poor, or, at the very least, ineffective teaching. He writes, "And just like adding a fertilizer, if the distribution of student learning after teaching resembles a normal bell-shaped curve, that, too, shows the degree to which our intervention failed. It made no difference." [18]

For teachers to buy into Guskey's argument and allow it to guide their grading practices, two things must be true. The first is that standards for excellence should remain high. The second is that grades should be given based on standards. This, of course, goes back to how one defines grades. If grades are being used to rank students, then a bell curve may be acceptable, but if grades are meant to report how students perform relative to a certain standard, be it a vague standard such as "excellence" or more specific criteria, then lots of high grades should not automatically be viewed with disdain or skepticism.

Guskey speaks to this as well in citing obstacle number one to grading reform as the belief that "grades should provide the basis for differentiating students." Here he writes that teachers should ask themselves, "Is my purpose to *select* talent or *develop* it?" He then explains that if your purpose is selecting talent, then you must work to "maximize the differences among students," thus creating a wide range of grades allowing you or other constituencies to easily differentiate students. However, Guskey is damning in his condemnation of this practice, writing that the "best means of maximizing differences in learning is poor teaching. Nothing does it better."[19]

On the other hand, if a teacher's goal is to develop talent rather than select it, he or she will provide clear explanations of the standards and then do everything possible to help each student get there, in which case higher achievement across the board is a positive thing.

So what is the purpose of teaching, to select talent or to develop it? The answer seems clear, and it has already been suggested in this book that the task of sorting students should be left to colleges and those who have a more vested interest in differentiating between students. A teacher should be pleased if colleges have a difficult time differentiating between students because they have all achieved so highly. Further, if standardized tests are not doing the job effectively, then perhaps colleges could move toward looking at portfolios of work or adding more weight to interviews and recommendation letters, things that undoubtedly will tell them more about a student than grades and test scores.

PRACTICAL CONCERNS

Keeping Standards Consistent and High

Although getting all of one's students to achieve highly should be every teacher's goal, it would be naive to say that lots of As in a grade distribution automatically means that great teaching is occurring and that all students are performing highly. Undoubtedly, a critic may say to this whole argument, the problem is not one of too much high achievement (that would be fine); the problem is high grades being given for achievement that is not high. As stated earlier, high grades should not be given when they are undeserved, so we must find ways to make sure they are deserved, and those solutions are clearer standards, standards-based grading, and improved consistency in grading.

Student Motivation

Critics may also claim that grades based on standards that do less to differentiate students will diminish student motivation because it is the competition for those few As that drives students or the scarcity of As that creates the demand for them. One solution to this is to stop thinking in terms of As and to think instead of meeting and exceeding standards. Students then compete against themselves to reach various levels of achievement. As in any grading system, some students will push themselves, and some will not, and if standards of achievement remain high, diligent students will continue to toil to meet and exceed them, just as they had toiled for those few As.

Let us also not forget that, as suggested in chapter 2, motivation based on a desire for high grades is antithetical to the deep and lasting motivation that will result in lifelong learning.

Feedback

A more realistic problem with a compressed grade distribution that does less to differentiate among students is whether or not students receive useful feedback on their performance, which is one of the important pedagogical purposes for giving grades. While As, Bs, Cs, and Ds are limited in the specificity of the feedback that they can give, the wider range can perhaps better allow students to accurately perceive where they stand. This is why telling students that they meet or exceed standards is not enough. The standards should clearly define what students should know and be able to do, and teachers should rate their performance on each element of the curriculum, giving them a much clearer picture of their performance than any number and letter could do.

THE IMPORTANCE OF FAILURE

Those fighting against grade inflation or higher grades feel that school is getting easier or that students are not being held as accountable as they should be. They would likely attribute this to too much concern for student self-esteem, which results in a reluctance to allow students to fail. Although the case has already been made that higher grades do not automatically mean that standards have been lowered, still one must wonder if all this success is a good thing. After all, much current research speaks to the importance of failure in building grit and resiliency—two traits linked closely to overall success in life.[20]

If failure is, in fact, valuable, then the challenge is to create conditions in which failure is acceptable and leads to growth, rather than ones in which failure instills a fixed mindset in students and puts them on a track from which they cannot recover. Fs and grading systems that rank student performance do the latter, whereas grading against a standard should tell a student who fails, "You're not there yet, but keep working hard and you can get there." Teachers might feel more comfortable failing students if it is clearer that they are not actually labeling the student a failure, but simply indicating that his or her performance is not yet where it needs to be.

In *The Genius in All of Us*, David Shenk, drawing on James Flynn's research, reports that 98 percent of those who take the IQ test today score better than the average test taker in 1900.[21] Human intelligence and skills seem to have increased. This is a good thing, and it is exactly what we should want to see in our classrooms. Perhaps this would mean that it is time to make the standards of achievement higher, but once we do, we should keep working until once again, we are faced with the "problem" of too many high grades.

In reality, there will never be all As. Some students will not work hard, and some will not be able to reach that level in the given time constraint. But excellence should remain the goal for all students. After all, an A in a high school class should not actually require genius—maybe genius isn't in all of us, as Shenk's title suggests, but As in school just might be.

NOTES

1. Stuart Rojstaczer and Christopher Healy, "Where A Is Ordinary: The Evolution of American College and University Grading, 1940–2009," *Teachers College Record* 114.7 (2012): 1–23. Also see Katherine Rampell, "A History of College Grade Inflation," *New York Times*, July 14, 2011.

2. Mark Bauerlein, "A Is for 'All Too Common': Rampant College Grade Inflation Is a Real Economic Problem," *New York Daily News*, July 24, 2011, http://www.nydailynews.com/opinion/common-rampant-college-grade-inflation-real-economic-problem-article-1.156828.

3. Phillip Babcock and Mindy Marks, "The Falling Time Cost of College: Evidence from Half a Century of Time Use Data," *Review of Economics and Statistics*, 93.2 (2011): 468–478.

4. James Flynn, *Are We Getting Smarter? Rising IQ in the Twenty-First Century* (Cambridge: Cambridge University Press, 2012), 1.

5. Karen Anderson, "Students Receive Fewer A's and Princeton Calls It Progress," *New York Times*, September 20, 2005, http://www.nytimes.com/2005/09/20/nyregion/20grades.html?_r=1&.

6. David Shenk, *The Genius in All of Us* (New York: Doubleday, 2010), 10.

7. Ibid.

8. Alfred Binet, *Modern Ideas about Children*, 105–106, quoted in *Handbook of Competence and Motivation*, edited by Andrew Elliot and Carol Dweck (New York: Guilford, 2009), 124.

9. Ibid.

10. Shenk, *The Genius in All of Us*, 33–34.

11. Robert J. Sternberg, "Intelligence Competence and Expertise," in *Handbook of Competence and Motivation*, edited by Andrew Elliot and Carol Dweck (New York: Guilford, 2009), 18, quoted in Shenk, *The Genius in All of Us*, 42.

12. Sternberg, "Intelligence," 21, quoted in Shenk, *The Genius in All of Us*, 185.

13. Carol Dweck, *Mindset: The New Psychology of Success* (New York: Ballantine, 2006).

14. Thomas R. Guskey, "Five Obstacles to Grading Reform," *Educational Leadership* 69.3 (2011): 18.

15. Ibid.

16. Ibid.

17. Ibid.

18. Ibid.

19. Ibid., 17.

20. For an overview of this research, see Paul Tough, "What if the Secret to Success Is Failure?" *New York Times Magazine*, September 14, 2011, http://www.nytimes.com/ 2011/09/ 18/magazine/what-if-the-secret-to-success-is-failure.html?pagewanted=all.

21. Shenk, *The Genius in All of Us*, 36.

Chapter 4

The Forms Grades Take: Numbers versus Letters

THE MOST COMMON FORMS

Part 1 of this book went to great lengths to provide the many possible ways to define a grade. Once a teacher, school, or school system has done that, they must then decide how they intend to represent their grades on assignments, report cards, and transcripts. As already pointed out in chapter 1, one's decision regarding the nature of information being conveyed will certainly lead in a particular direction regarding what form the grade will take. A quantification will certainly be a number, and a symbol will usually be a letter (generally between A and F, with the exception of E, which I assume was left out just to make it clearer to students who earned the lowest grade that they had *f*ailed).

Anyhow, these are the two most commonly used systems of grades, and they are often combined in systems that use numbers that equate to letters (97–100 = A+, 83–86 = B, etc.) or letters that convert to numbers in order to generate a traditional GPA (A = 4, B = 3, C = 2, D = 1, and F = 0). Thus, the three most common options for the form a grade may take are as follows:

1. A number
2. A letter
3. A number that equates to a letter or vice versa

PROBLEMS WITH THE 0–100 SCALE

Each one of these forms brings with it certain assumptions that affect the message that is conveyed by the grade, and because of this, each poses some problems. The most obvious problem with numbers when using a 0–100 scale is that the grade implies a percentage of material correct. Often this is, in fact, the case, such as when a student gets one question wrong on a ten-question quiz and receives a 90. In this situation, it would be quite appropriate for the teacher to write "90 percent" at the top of the assignment.

However, not all assignments can be broken down into percentages that easily, and as teachers begin to use more and more open-response, authentic assessments, this will even more frequently be the case. The clearest example is an essay. How is a teacher supposed to put a number between 0 and 100 on an essay? Imagine that a teacher just graded a quiz on which the grade reflected the percentage correct. Now how does he or she give a grade of the same form on an essay—how does the teacher determine the percentage of the essay that is correct?

The answer to that question is that it cannot be done. Writing assignments are not graded based on the percentage that is correct. Teachers may put a number on them that they feel is appropriate based on the overall quality of the essay, but this number should not be followed by a percentage sign. If these numbers are linked to letter grades, then it is simplified a bit since the letter grades imply general standards of achievement that the teacher can apply to his or her assessment of the essay. If this is the case, then the teacher may (and probably should) simply put the letter on the essay. However, in these situations a number usually still goes in the grade book so that it can be averaged with scores on quizzes and the like. This means the teacher ends up averaging a percentage-based grade and a standards-based grade, which may result in some fuzzy math.

The further problem is that even when numbers are tied to letters and they are not meant to reflect percentages, any time a number between 0 and 100 is used, our brains begin thinking in percentages. The result of thinking in terms of percentages is twofold. First, on written or open-response assignments, teachers are reluctant to give 100 (A+, for all intents and purposes). This is because 100 percent is associated with perfection. Many humanities teachers feel this way, even going so far as to say, "I will never give a 100 on a paper because there will always be at least one small mistake." Now, there is a difference between getting all of the answers correct on a quiz and writing a perfect paper. In order to earn the highest grade possible on an essay or open-response assignment while in middle or high school, one should not have to write like Ernest Hemingway or Jane Austen; the paper should simply be at the highest standard that can be expected for that grade level. However, because our minds link the number 100 to a percentage, our most skilled students often cannot earn A+ in humanities classes that require writing.

The second implication of thinking about number grades in terms of percentages is problematic at the other end of the spectrum. When using number grades from 0 to 100, even when they are tied to letters, an assignment that is not handed in earns a 0. Of course, on one level this makes sense—the student did not do the work, so he or she receives no credit. However, in practice this will skew the student's grade downward in an unfair and misleading way. A student has four assignments; she earns 100 on three of them and then does not hand in the fourth, earning a 0. This means that her average is 75 percent—a C performance in the class.

The math seems to work, but no one would suggest that this student's skills are at the C level. Of course, this does bring us back to the importance of clearly defining what grades mean in one's class and one's school. To give this student a 75 or a C is not a representation of her skill level or mastery of the course material; it represents some combination of skill and responsibility or work ethic. If one wants this to be the case, that is acceptable, but it must be clearly stated.

Still, even if this is the case, the math remains misleading. The above scenario, with three scores of 100 and one score of 0 heavily weights the grade toward responsibility and work ethic over academic skill. From a statistical perspective, giving 0s tremendously skews what grades are supposed to represent, particularly in systems that equate numbers and letters. Generally A is in the 90s, B in the 80s, C in the 70s, D in the 60s, and F anywhere below that. Now, if each letter grade has a range of ten points, except F, which has a range of 60, earning an F can carry more weight than earning an A. The best grade one can earn (100) is only 25 points above a C (the median grade in the range), whereas the worst grade one can earn (0) is 75 points below that median. Clearly this system does not make sense mathematically.

Many schools have addressed this problem by instituting a floor for grades; for example, prohibiting teachers from giving grades lower than 50. This makes a great deal of sense: if A through D each get a ten-point range, why shouldn't the same thing be true for F? Critics of this theory will point to that assignment that was not handed in and say, how can you give students any credit at all for doing nothing? They do not deserve fifty points; they deserve nothing.

On its face, this argument makes sense, which again points to a flaw in the 0–100 system of grading. It would work if F were 0–20, D 21–40, C 41–60, and so on, but that is generally not the case. A floor grade suggests that 50 is actually 0. That is the lowest students can get, and if that is the case, then they are not getting something for nothing; they are getting nothing—50 just happens to equal nothing. The fact that this is so confusing and counterintuitive is a good reason to abandon the 0–100 scale.

It is worth noting another point that will be raised in this debate, which is that a student who does the work and tries his or her best but fails should not get the same grade as a student who does not do the work. This would be cited as a good explanation for the difference between a 0 and 50. It's plausible to say that the floor grade for work completed should be 50, but if you do not hand in the work, then you earn a 0. That makes sense, but again, it comes back to how one defines grades, since, as indicated above, the student who earns As on the work he or she hands in but doesn't hand in some work will get a grade that reflects things other than academic ability. In fact, if one's grades are meant to represent academic ability or performance, then the student who does all of the work but cannot pass should have a lower grade than the student with the strong skills but inconsistent work ethic. This is not to say that one is more appropriate than the other, but just to point out the differences and again highlight the importance of first defining what one's grades are meant to represent before choosing a system.

THE PROBLEM WITH NUMBER-LETTER EQUIVALENCY

Further problems occur when using a 0–100 scale that is tied to letter grades in a system of number-letter equivalency. Again, generally assume that As are in the 90s, Bs in the 80s, and so on. Let us say a teacher gives a five-question quiz, which she naturally plans to grade with a 0–100 scale, viewing the number as a percentage of correct material (even though, as we saw above, this cannot always be the case). On this quiz, a well-prepared, diligent, and highly skilled student gets one question wrong. What does he get? An 80—in this case probably labeled with a percentage, because he did in fact get 80 percent correct. However, this 80, based on just one mistake, gets this student a low B, almost a C. If the student had gotten two wrong, then he or she would have essentially failed. Perhaps this says more about the questionable pedagogy of giving quizzes of this nature, but it does point out the tenuous link between numbers (often seen as percentages) and what the letters that they equate to commonly represent.

Of course, one only runs into this problem on assessments that ask for some objective answer—assessments on which the percentage of correct material can, in fact, be measured. However, most other assessments—papers, projects, and presentations—cannot be graded as a percentage of correct material; yet, in grading systems that use numbers between 0 and 100, a teacher is still required to select a number. He or she might (and should) avoid the issue by simply putting a letter grade on whatever he or she gives back to the student (if the system is one of number-letter equivalency). Yet, at the end of the day, if an average is required of the teacher for the summative grade, then he or she will have to put a number in the grade book.

One must acknowledge that there is some arbitrariness in doing so. A teacher will pick a number that fits the range for that letter grade, but really what's the difference between a 92 and a 93? Not much. But on the other hand, there is a big difference between and 80 and 79 because that may be the difference between a B and a C. Thus, selecting 92 as opposed to 93 on that essay could have been what took the student's average from 80 to 79. One might argue that if the student is a B student, and you know it, then just give that person the 80 or B−, regardless of what the numbers say. Great idea—then why use numbers in the first place?

There is one way, however, to try to make numbers on subjective, open-ended assignments work, and that is through the use of a rubric with point values assigned to the various standards and expectations for that particular assignment. For example, an essay might get 25 points for each of the following four areas: (1) ideas, (2) evidence, (3) organization, and (4) grammar and mechanics. In this case, the teacher could literally take a point away from the 25 in the grammar and mechanics section for each mistake made. However, there remain some problems with this method. A student who makes 25 mistakes would get 0 points—no credit for grammar and mechanics, when he or she undoubtedly had some sentences that were written without error, so this does not fit the standard of percentage of correct material for which numbers seem to work. Furthermore, in the sections other than grammar and mechanics, choosing a number remains somewhat arbitrary. What level of organization earns 23 points? How is that different from 22 or 24?

Even if one feels comfortable with this and likes the idea of being able to break down an assessment and quantify different areas, which can be helpful for a student in understanding his or her performance, often the sum total or final grade does not seem to reflect the overall quality of the piece. Teachers find themselves in situations where the numbers add up to 78/C+, but they really feel that the work deserved a B. Hence, we see the disconnect between a numerical label on an essay or other open-response assessment and a teacher's general sense of the quality of the work (for more on the topic of rubrics see chapter 12).

A FINAL NOTE ON THE 0–100 SCALE

This may all have seemed like a moot point to those who give only assessments that have clear right and wrong answers, for which 0–100 as a percentage of correct material works just fine. However, it is worth noting that exclusively giving assessments of this nature is poor practice in the twenty-first century. Grading will certainly become a lot more challenging when one begins to give authentic, open-ended performance-based assessments, and that is why we must put so much thought into this process.

THE CASE FOR LETTERS

Given all that has just been said about the complications of numbers and the ways in which they can be misleading, inaccurate, and arbitrary, it seems as though letters are a more appropriate form for grades. They take some of the fuzzy math out of the equation in terms of 0s and averaging, and they are more easily defined in terms of aligning them with general or particular standards of performance.

Certainly, one may ask, "How exactly do you average letters without aligning them with numbers?" This is a good question. If one still feels compelled to use a 0–100 scale and to combine assessments that have been given letter grades with ones that are graded based on percentage correct, then one could select a number for each letter. For example A = 95, B = 85, C = 75, D = 65, and F = 55. This takes out the arbitrariness of selecting between, say, an 82 and an 81.

One may still argue that this is not specific enough because there are distinctions between student performances within the category defined by one letter, and that all those numbers allow a teacher to make distinctions. However, teachers do have the option of using the common plus and minus designations along with a letter, and of assigning specific numbers for plus and minus between the ones assigned to each letter. It may be enough to have one mark between each letter, as in A−/B+ = 90, as opposed to separate grades for A− and B+, which can slide toward arbitrariness. However, the point is that the letter should come first, not the number, because it is the letter that is aligned to the standard. After all, it is hard to imagine assigning a different standard of performance to each number between 50 and 100.

What this helps teachers to avoid is a situation in which the following thought process occurs: "Well, I gave that last project an A, which equated to a 95, and while this one is good and deserves an A, it just wasn't quite as good as the last one, so I will give this one a 94." The problem here is that the teacher has begun grading by ranking as opposed to assessing the work that has been done against a standard. If certain criteria for performance have been articulated for each grade level, then it does not matter if one is a little better than another; what matters in determining the grade is whether or not a defined standard of performance is met. Of course, no two As will be exactly the same, and one may be slightly better than another, but they are alike in that they both meet the same predetermined standards. This takes out the hairsplitting and hopefully the subjectivity of comparing one assignment to another. Perhaps another teacher may think the opposite about the two pieces of work, and while there will always be some subjectivity in grading, this might help to reduce it.

SOME CONCERNS ABOUT LETTERS

Clearly, this argument suggests that for assignments that do not have clear right and wrong answers, letter grades are more effective. However, there are still some issues with the standard A–F scale. The problem is the baggage that these letters have from years of use across multiple generations. Traditionally, Cs have come to be defined as average, and this designation brings with it a host of problems. The first is that the term *average* implies that one is grading students relative to one another and that grade distribution should be a bell curve. This notion was dismantled in chapter 3. However, the notion of C as average has persisted, even when it is not mathematically the case. In certain schools, a C is far from an average grade and is much more akin to failure. In fact, when trying to get into a top-tier college, a C on one's transcript may be the death knell. Yet at the same time, because of the historical understanding of a C, a student who may very well have gotten the worst grade in the class can say, "I didn't do that badly. I got a C—that's average. It's not like I got a D or an F. I'm doing okay."

ALTERNATIVE GRADING SYSTEMS

As was pointed out in chapter 3, teachers should not feel badly about using only the higher range of the traditional grading scale, but the baggage associated with it suggests that perhaps it is time for a new scale. In fact, there is good reason to create one's own scale in order to make students and parents pay attention to what it actually means, instead of just making assumptions based on previous experience. These systems may be different letters, an alternate range of numbers, or even symbols. It matters less what the system is than how clearly defined the various standards of performance are. If one's system requires an average at the end of the marking period, then the system will have to be translated into numbers at some point, but these need not be 0–100. The traditional 0–4 number scale (often used to calculate GPA) is an example of this, and is a pretty sound system, except that it carries a great deal of baggage because of its alignment with the A–F scale. Nevertheless, chapter 5 examines whether or not averages are needed and in what situations they are appropriate.

Keep in mind that grades need not come in the form of symbols. They can be written descriptions of standards. These may not seem like grades at all— and what an interesting notion that is, since such a system would get students and parents to think less about grades and more about the actual learning and improvement of skills that is occurring in and out of the classroom. This is easy to do on individual assignments, where one can simply provide a detailed and descriptive standards-based rubric, but what about summative grades? We will also turn to this question as we examine the weighting and averaging of grades in chapter 5.

Chapter 5

Determining Summative Grades

WHAT ARE SUMMATIVE GRADES?

Chapter 4 examined the various forms a grade can take, mainly in terms of grades on individual assignments. While the same principles may apply to the forms of summative grades, how one uses grades from multiple assignments to arrive at a summative grade merits a discussion of its own. A summative grade can be defined as any grade that uses data from multiple assessments in an attempt to give an overall report of a student's learning, skills, performance, or progress over a defined period of time. Summative grades generally come in the form of term, semester, or year grades, but could refer to a grade for a unit of study, an assignment with multiple parts, or multiple standards, each given a different score.

In determining summative grades there are three overlapping questions to consider: (1) how to combine them; (2) how to weight them; and (3) what to count and what not to count. As is the case throughout this book, answers to these questions should all be determined by how the teachers or schools have chosen to define grades and for what purpose they are using them. Nevertheless, let us consider the possibilities and implications of the various decisions that can be made.

It is worth noting that to combine grades in a meaningful way, they generally have to be in the form of numbers, so even if a teacher uses another form for grades, having a number equivalent makes it easier to determine an accurate summative grade.

METHODS OF COMBINING GRADES: AVERAGING AND WEIGHTING

The most common way to combine grades is by averaging them. Add the scores and divide by the number of assessments, and voilà, you have your summative grade. This method assumes that all assessments should play an equal role in determining a student's summative grade. Generally though, teachers do not feel this is the case and choose to weight assignments differently. This can be accomplished with one of the following methods:

1. Assigning a specific percentage of the overall grade to each assignment (Teachers sometimes reflect this by referring to the "amount of points something is worth.")
2. Averaging assignments within categories, with each category making up a certain percentage of the grade
3. Combining the above

Assigning a specific percentage of the overall grade to each assignment results in a menu with infinite variations of tests, homework assignments, quizzes, essays, presentations, and projects, all worth a range of different points based on how significant the teacher feels each assignment is. Add up the total points earned and divide by the total points possible, and you have a student's "average," even if not technically a calculated mean.

The second method establishes categories with predetermined weights (e.g., tests 50 percent, quizzes 25 percent, homework 15 percent, class participation 10 percent). Assignments are averaged with those in their category, and that average is multiplied by its weight and then added to the results of other categories, yielding the summative grade. The two methods can be combined by giving assignments relative weights within their category—in essence practicing the first method of "earned points/total points" within a category and then weighting the categories as well.

It is important to note that both of these systems will give you a number out of 100, but that neither are, strictly speaking, averages, despite the fact that students and teachers will often refer to them as such. Also, remember that when you are dealing with numbers out of 100, people will often make an intuitive leap to refer to them as percentages, but, as suggested in chapter 4, this does not necessarily, and in most cases will not, mean percentage of material correct. It is important to avoid this confusion for all of the reasons stated in chapter 4.

So what are the different implications of these two systems? The former system, which we will refer to as the total points system, does not require teachers to plan ahead in terms of knowing exactly how many and what types of assessments they will give. The teacher can decide as he or she goes how many points an assignment is worth based on what has come before. With the weighted categories, teachers need an assessment plan clearly laid out beforehand in order to make sure that the relative weights of individual assignments are appropriate.

If in the above example, where tests are worth 50 percent of the summative grade and quizzes are worth 25 percent, for some reason the teacher gives four tests but only two quizzes, then each individual test and quiz end up being worth the same thing, making the quizzes count just as much as the tests. While the flexibility afforded by the total points system is convenient, one can certainly argue that teachers should have a comprehensive assessment plan going into a marking period. Doing so gives them the ability to more clearly determine the relative importance of each assignment so that the grade most accurately reflects the students' performance or skills in critical areas of the course.

The other issue to consider is the element of transparency for the students. If each assignment has a clearly indicated point value, as would be the case with the total point system, then students will be well aware of its impact on their grades relative to other assignments. With the weighted categories, the relative weight of each individual assignment may not be as readily apparent to them. However, with a clear assessment plan, this does not have to be the case, since teachers can be very open about what the categories are worth and how many assignments there will be in each category. That being the case, a teacher could tell a student exactly what percentage of the summative grade each assignment is worth. Although teachers should be transparent about grades, they must be careful not to cultivate an attitude in which students consider assessments not as learning opportunities, but merely as percentages of grades.

Thus, one wonders if ensuring that students know exactly how much an assignment contributes to their grade is antithetical to learning. The term *importance* was not used when discussing the point allotment or weight of an assignment or category because students should not be led to draw a correlation between the importance of an assignment and its impact on their grade. A given homework assignment (although it may not be as large a factor in the determination of a summative grade) may be no less important to the learning process than a test. Students should approach all of their work as if it is important and as if they have potential to learn something from it.

WEIGHTING EVERY ASSIGNMENT THE SAME

The line of thinking outlined at the conclusion of the previous section might suggest that one should forget about weighting assignments and determine an average by counting each assignment—the short homework assignment, the unit-ending test, and the lengthy research paper—exactly the same. While this method has many flaws, which shall be discussed, it has the following merits: every assignment matters, but no assignment matters too much (which is an appropriate attitude to take toward most things in life). This means that students should approach each assignment with a seriousness of purpose, but also with an awareness that no single assignment will make or break their grade. Such an attitude could foster the risk taking and innovation that teachers would like to see more of from their students.

Despite these merits, a system of determining a summative grade for a student based upon an average in which all assignments count equally has a number of flaws. If, for example, one wishes the grade to be an accurate representation of a student's skill level in certain areas, then his or her performance on particular assignments—generally culminating assessments for given units of study—should be weighted more heavily since it is designed to give the teacher the very information he or she wishes the grade to represent. This is not the case with other assignments that may be less challenging, more limited in scope, or used as building blocks to something larger and more comprehensive. In short, averaging every assignment a student completes and counting them all equally may not give teachers the information that they actually desire the grade to represent.

Another flaw with the method that counts everything the same is that it flies in the face of using formative assessments as practice for the summative assessments. This is particularly important when introducing students to a new concept or skill. You may wish to grade their performances early on in order to give them a sense of where they stand relative to the standard, but it seems only fitting that early assessments in a unit, be they homework assignments or quizzes, not be given as much weight toward the summative grade as a culminating assessment—one for which students have had ample practice and preparation.

USING THE MEDIAN AND THE MODE

Another issue with averaging grades is that the teacher may not actually want the grade to represent an average. If this is the case, a teacher may wish to consider using the median or the mode (as opposed to the mean) in determining a summative grade. Using the median diminishes the impact of outlier or aberrant performances, both positive and negative. If a student generally earns grades in the B range but gets one zero (or whatever the school's minimum grade is), then the median will still be a B, whereas that low grade might pull the mean into the C range. Yes, that would be the average, but it might not be as accurate a representation of his or her skills. In fact, using a median instead of a mean makes minimum grade policies less relevant and would allow zeroes to be given without unfairly skewing the grade as they do when calculated as part of a mean.

Using the mode would likely achieve a similar result, although it is not as practical, particularly with number grades, since the exact same grade is unlikely to recur with frequency. However, with letter grades the mode is certainly worth paying attention to. If on six assignments a student earned three Fs, two Bs, and one A, he or she might not deserve an F as the summative grade, but it would be worth pointing out that F was the most commonly occurring grade.

One may also combine these systems, for example by using the median or mode within categories that are weighted relative to other categories.

DROPPING THE LOWEST GRADE

If using the median or mode to determine a summative grade serves to lessen the impact of outlier grades, so does the common policy of dropping the lowest grade. This only eliminates grades that are outliers in a negative direction—making the practice very popular among students. It does make a great deal of sense if grades are meant to represent a student's skill level and one wishes to account for the fact that everyone has a bad day. This practice also helps to create a situation in which students are more willing to take risks and attempt innovation, since they know they can fail once without detriment to their grade.

However, it does not make as much sense to use this practice if it can apply to any assessment and the assessments are weighted differently. An extreme example would be that of a student failing a final exam and having that grade dropped. Clearly, this would not result in a grade that was an accurate representation of the student's learning, skill, performance, or progress. This policy makes the most sense when it allows for a grade to be dropped from a series of similar assessments—the lowest homework grade, the lowest quiz score, or even the lowest test score if there are a number of tests. One can even imagine a scenario in which the lowest score is dropped from each category that includes a large number of assignments.

That said, teachers should use discretion when applying this practice. The point of it is to throw out aberrant grades so that a student's grade is more accurate; the point is not just to boost students' grades in an effort to be nice or make them feel good. Thus, any assessment that provides critical data should not be dropped. Furthermore, the practice of dropping the lowest grade makes much more sense in classes in which all of the assessments are skills-based rather than content-based. If a student writes a series of analytical essays in an English class, then it is unlikely that any one essay performance provides more critical data than another.

However, in a physics class, where the tests are on different topics, such as mechanics, electricity, and magnetism, a student's performance on each represents something very different, and hence, to drop one score would seem inappropriate given that the grade should represent a student's understanding of all areas of physics.

Keep in mind that when it comes to formative assessments, one should feel comfortable not counting them at all if they are designed as practice for the culminating assessment. This is very different than dropping grades on assessments that were intended to provide the teacher with data for the summative grade.

WEIGHTING TOWARD THE MOST RECENT PERFORMANCE

Another idea to consider is using summative grades that are more heavily weighted toward students' skill level at the time when the summative grade is assigned. This idea suggests that the most recent work is what should count the most, and perhaps is all that matters. After all, what difference does it make that a student didn't know something or couldn't do something in the past if he or she knows or can do it in the present?

Averaging all grades in skills-based courses could punish students for starting at a lower place or for progressing more slowly than other students. Imagine that when summative grades are reported, two students have an equal skill level, but two weeks earlier one's skill level was a lot lower. It seems, if anything, that the performance of the person who maybe earned grades of C, B, and A (in that order) is more impressive than the student who earned three As. Again, it all comes down to how one defines grades. A grade that rewards students in the manner just suggested would be one that attempted to report on student progress.

As with dropping the lowest grade, this theory does not work when the different assessments represent knowledge or understanding of different things or performance of different skills. Science and history classes seem to be disciplines in which all units need to count toward the summative grade since each unit represents knowledge and understanding of a different thing. In English, world languages, and math, skill level is what matters, and you simply cannot progress without gaining proficiency in previous skills, so ability and performance in the past is less relevant than ability in the present.

WHEN TO GIVE SUMMATIVE GRADES

Generally, summative grades are given at the end of marking periods—terms, quarters, trimesters, semesters, and years, depending on a particular school's calendar. A question to consider with regard to the assigning of summative grades at these points is whether or not the summative grade for a marking period (other than the final marking period for a course, be it a semester or a full year) should be fixed. Should a semester grade be the average of two quarters, or should that first quarter be an indicator grade of where that student stands at the halfway point of the term? Schools that give midterm grades often use them in that manner. This method seems more consistent with allowing students the opportunity to grow and improve, and allows the potential for the summative grade to be weighted toward performance on the most recent assessments.

Further, one may even consider whether or not a grade for a term within a larger calendar should ever be permanent. When we consider rewrites and retakes later in the book, scenarios may arise in which students continue to work on an assignment even after a marking period has passed, and one must make decisions about whether to allow summative grades that have already been reported to be changed. To avoid this problem one can make sure all rewrites and retakes are completed before the end of a marking period, but one should never let the schedule for grade reporting stand in the way of encouraging further learning.

DETERMINING GRADE POINT AVERAGES

One last point that needs to be addressed in this chapter is the determining of GPAs, which take summative grades from different classes and combine them in an attempt to label a student's overall academic performance. Obviously, any single number or letter is completely reductive and provides very little specific information about a student's academic performance. Mainly these are used to rank and sort students for colleges, neither of which serve any pedagogical benefit. Therefore, there is little purpose in discussing GPAs here, other than to point out that they are an attempt to lump data about widely different things into one number and hence are of little educational value to a student. Yes, they will tell you if a student is generally high or low achieving, but this reductivism only encourages a focus on grades instead of learning and on results instead of process, both of which are antithetical to genuine academic achievement.

Chapter 6

Grading and Failure

THE IMPORTANCE OF LEARNING TO OVERCOME FAILURE

The work of Paul Tough, highlighted by his much-circulated *New York Times Magazine* article, "What if the Secret to Success Is Failure?" and his book *How Children Succeed: Grit, Curiosity, and the Hidden Power of Character*, underscores what many educators long have known—it is good for students to fail once in a while.[1] Yes, confidence and self-esteem are important, but to swing too far in that direction and do everything in our power to ensure that students never experience failure does a great disservice to them.

It is almost inevitable that, when they are adults, our students will fail at something. It is much better that they have this experience in school first so that when it happens to them in their professional or personal lives, they are more equipped to deal with it. According to Tough and Angela Duckworth, upon whose research Tough relies, the character trait needed to successfully deal with failure is grit, and the only way students will develop grit is by practicing it—being put into situations where they fail and then are forced overcome that failure. Overcoming failure is not something that just happens. Allowing students to experience failure is only one part of it; they also need to be given the opportunity to bounce back and overcome this adversity, and they must be coached and guided along the way.

ALLOWING STUDENTS TO FAIL VERSUS FAILING STUDENTS

Grades seem an obvious way to allow students to experience failure. However, there is a difference between allowing students to fail and failing one's students. The former implies putting them in situations in which they do not have immediate success, and providing them with the support that they need to learn from and overcome this failure. The latter simply means giving them failing grades, and if this is all teachers do, then they are failing their students in an even greater sense of the phrase.

So how does one allow students to fail without failing them? Teachers need to create safe spaces in which students can fail in the short term but bounce back over time. If teachers simply give students failing grades, but neither allow them to overcome nor guide them toward overcoming this failure, then little has been done to help them. Critics might argue that if we allow students the opportunity to bounce back from failure, then we have not really allowed them to experience failure. This line of reasoning is the result of confusion over the meaning of the very term *failure*.

For some reason, when it comes to education, people seem to think that failure must be absolute. In this view, to fail a student equates to a form of eternal damnation, and any redemption they are allowed means they did not, in fact, fail. Yet in the real world—what Paul Tough wants all students to be prepared for—failure is not so eternal. In the real world, failure is a setback, something that we can overcome by putting our minds to it. If your novel does not get published, you can revise it, resubmit it, or write another one— you are not forbidden ever to put pen to paper again. If you lose your job, you pick yourself up and go out and get another one—you are not condemned to a life of unemployment. If your sales pitch does not work on a certain customer, you fine-tune it and try it on someone else.

The adage "what doesn't kill you only makes you stronger" applies per- fectly here. In a nutshell, this is what Tough is arguing—adolescents need to fail because they will likely become stronger for having had the experience— but again, this is only true if they are coached, guided, and given opportu- nities to overcome the failure. After all, what doesn't kill you makes you stronger, whereas what kills you, well, kills you.

While acceptance to a certain college should by no means be the measure of learning, the fact of the matter is that in today's age of high-stakes college admissions, failing a class just may kill your chances of being admitted to a top-tier college. Getting an F on a major assignment that results in your getting a D in a class might do the same. Thus, getting any grade that results in an inability to have success in a class is not a situation in which a student can learn from failure.

Chapter 4 mentioned the concept of "floor" grades based on the statistical problems created by zeroes in a traditional grading scale in which every other letter grade gets a ten-point range and F gets 60 points. A discussion of the importance of learning from failure suggests more evidence for such floor grades so that students can recover as opposed to having a zero that essential- ly decimates their average, making success, at least as measured in the tradi- tional fashion, impossible.

The situation that seems to be ideal is one in which teachers can put an F (or whatever equivalent mark may exist) on student work, giving students a clear indication that they did, in fact, fail in the given task, while at the same time allowing them, through hard work and alternative strategies, to overcome such failure. Floor grades are just one way of attempting to create a situation in which this may occur. However, such policies may not go far enough in providing opportunities to show grit and resiliency in order to overcome failure.

THE CASE FOR REDOS, RETAKES, AND REWRITES

The spirit of the importance of allowing students to fail is much more about letting them know, candidly and bluntly, that their work was no good—their ideas did not make sense, they did not solve the problem, or the method they used was not effective. A way to give students this experience and allow them to build resiliency is through allowing redos, retakes, and rewrites.

Critics of this practice will say that allowing students to retake tests, redo projects, and rewrite papers is a reason why students will be ill-equipped to deal with failure. This is not the case. Rick Wormeli explains in an essay defending the practice of retakes and redos:

> How pompous is it for a teacher then, to declare to students, "This quiz/writing assignment/project/test cannot be redone for full credit because such a policy prepares you best for the working world." This teacher doesn't have a pedagogical leg to stand on. [In actuality,] the best preparation for the world beyond school is to learn essential content and skills well. [2]

What teachers who do not support retakes and rewrites want is accountability. They will argue that if a student does not do well on an assessment but is allowed to make up for that later, he or she is not being held accountable. But one wonders, is this really the way the world works?

Wormeli explains further: "The teacher who claims to be preparing students for the working world by disallowing all redos forgets that adult professionals actually flourish through redos, retakes and do-overs."[3] He then offers the following examples:

> LSAT. MCAT. Praxis. SAT. Bar exam. CPA exam. Driver's licensure. Pilot's licensure. Auto mechanic certification. Every one of these assessments reflects the adult-level, working world responsibilities our students will one day face. Many of them are high stakes: People's lives depend on these tests' validity as accurate measures of individual competence. All of them can be redone over and over *for full credit*. [4]

Students are not held accountable when they are given grades that they did not earn, but, as in the situations offered by Wormeli, allowing someone to show at a later date that he or she has gained proficiency or mastery is something completely different. In fact, many believe that such high stakes are involved in grading that teachers may be afraid to let their students fail, and give a mediocre grade even when it hasn't been earned to avoid overly negative consequences for the student. That is an example of not holding a student accountable, whereas telling students, "You failed, but I will allow you to try again," holds them accountable, allows them to experience true failure, and allows them to practice grit and resiliency so that they may have success and learn from their failure.

MAINTAINING ACCOUNTABILITY

Before moving on to discuss methods for implementing redo, retake, and rewrite policies, one caveat must be added about accountability. The situation that should most concern teachers is one in which students put no effort into an assignment or do not prepare at all for an assessment, but suffer no negative repercussions for their lack of effort because of a redo policy. Teachers are correct to guard against such a situation since this student has not learned from failure. If the student did not try or did not complete the work, then technically he or she did not fail and hence should not be offered another attempt—the student should face serious and lasting repercussions for this lack of effort. So, in instituting any redo, retake, or rewrite policy, the first rule must be that in order for a student to take advantage of such a policy, the teacher must judge that he or she put in a good-faith effort on the first attempt. How high a bar teachers set for this is up to their discretion, so long as the spirit of this rule is abided by.

IMPLEMENTING A REDO POLICY

Requiring a good-faith effort on the initial attempt is one rule that will hopefully go a long way toward easing the fears of the skeptics of such a policy, but there are also a number of other steps teachers can take to ensure that in implementing such a policy they are maintaining rigorous standards and creating a situation in which students truly do learn from failure. For example, there is a difference between simply correcting the mistakes that a teacher points out and truly reworking an assignment, whether it is a question on a test, a project, or an essay. The latter is what students must do if they wish to earn a higher grade on their second attempt at an assessment. If students are asked not just to correct mistakes but literally to redo their work, then and only then will they begin to learn from failure. That's resiliency.

That's what it means to stick with it and keep trying, and that is why teachers should consider allowing students to redo, retake, and rewrite. After all, how can students learn what it means to stick with something, to keep working at something until they get it right or until it comes out the way they want it to, if they are told, "You failed, too bad—now we are moving on to the next thing"?

To ensure that the redo process is rigorous and that it requires more than correcting mistakes, the teacher can build in a number of requirements and expectations that will make sure this is the case. The first is requiring students to complete a "redo justification memo." Such a document is essentially an application to redo one's work and might include both articulating an understanding of why it was that they earned the grade that they did, and providing an outline of what they intend to do or have done in order to improve. Whether a teacher has the student hand this in ahead of time or along with the redone work, it adds a hoop to jump through in order to make sure that students are serious about redoing the work. It forces them to assess where they went wrong and to articulate a clear strategy for improvement—exactly the steps anyone should engage in when hoping to overcome a failure.

In addition to the redo justification memo, a student should be required to resubmit the original work and to indicate through whatever means necessary what has been changed, added, or omitted in the revised attempt. On an essay, this may entail using, for example, a word-processing "track changes" function so that all changes are readily apparent to the teacher. This should make it easy for the teacher to determine, at just a glance, whether or not the work has been substantially altered. If it has not, then the student receives no additional credit.

A legitimate concern with such a policy is the additional grading it would require of a teacher. Thus, its feasibility will be different depending on how many students one has and how many assessments one gives. While ideally this policy would be open to all, and would allow students multiple opportunities to redo their work, if necessary for practical reasons, there are a number of ways in which a teacher can attempt to stop the volume of grading from becoming overwhelming. One such method would be to allow only those who earn below a certain level to redo their work. Again, in theory it would be better to allow all students to redo any work they wanted to, since failure can be relative, and we should never dissuade students from wanting to do something better.

Yet this simply may not be realistic, so it is perfectly acceptable to say that students who exhibit mastery or proficiency (or whatever grades are used to reflect those standards) are not allowed to redo their work, meaning that in this case it would truly be reserved only for those who had failed in a more objective sense. A teacher could also limit students to one redo per assignment. Again, this may not be ideal in theory but may be necessary for practical purposes. Finally, redos can never be unlimited because terms and marking periods end, and a student must redo work by a date that leaves the teacher enough time to grade it before summative grades are due. Teachers can and should set these deadlines leaving themselves ample time to get their grading done.

HOW TO GRADE REDOS

The central question regarding how to grade work that has been redone is, should the new grade stand or should it be averaged with the previous attempt? Wormeli answers with an analogy: suppose a runner wishes to qualify for the Olympics. Early in his career his times were well below what he needed to qualify, but eventually he got faster. Wormeli asks, "can you imagine telling a runner that his earlier 68.74 seconds from two years ago would be averaged with his new and improved 51.03 seconds, and that this mash-up would be his official number?"[5] The answer is, of course not. Olympic coaches want to reward current skill and care little for what someone could or could not do in the past. Whether or not one wishes to abide by this philosophy of only counting the most recent or best performance in grading depends, again, on how that person has chosen to define grades. If a teacher states that grades are a representation of current skill level, then it is appropriate to disregard the failure and count only the redo.

Nevertheless, teachers may have a different definition for grades and may be reluctant to totally discount the original work. If this is the case, teachers may choose to average the grades on the different attempts, but they must understand that by doing so, they are valuing the speed at which a certain level of performance can be attained, and that distinctions in grades between students may reflect not discrepancies in skill level, but discrepancies in how quickly students were able to reach a certain skill level. This is a legitimate system, but it remains important that teachers are transparent about these issues.

Teachers may also wish to implement ceiling grades, setting a limit on how high a grade a student can earn on work that is redone. Another idea would be to count the original and the redo, but to use the median in determining the summative grade so that redos don't totally replace the impact of original work but are able to minimize it to a greater extent. Finally, depending on the school's system of reporting, perhaps there are ways in which current skill level is reported along with the number of attempts it took for a student to reach that level. Doing so would be an attempt to address those who would claim unfairness based on the fact that some students earned a certain level on a first attempt.

WHICH CLASSES SHOULD HAVE REDO POLICIES

The nature of the particular class will have a bearing on whether or not or to what extent a teacher implements a redo policy. If a class is essentially a skills-based course in which students work to develop the same skills over the course of the semester or year, then there is less of a need for such a policy. For example, in an upper-level English course that asks students to analyze literature throughout the year and get progressively better at doing so, there is not much reason for allowing a student to rewrite his essay on Jane Austen's *Pride and Prejudice* when during the next unit, he will have to write a similar essay—one that requires the same skills—on Shakespeare's *Hamlet*. In a course such as this, one would be perfectly justified in saying to a student, "Sorry, you failed your essay on Austen, but don't worry, you will get another shot when we study Shakespeare." Of course, the question of whether both essays should factor into the grade remains.

Notice that this only makes sense if the students are being assessed solely on skills. If one of the teacher's goals is to ensure that the students have a deep understanding of *Pride and Prejudice* and that they will need to build upon this understanding later in the course, then it makes more sense to allow a rewrite. This is definitely the case when different units require different skills, and is particularly so if proficiency in a previous unit is necessary to understand or complete a later unit. In such cases, it almost seems imperative that the teacher institutes measures to make sure students gain proficiency before progressing too much further in the curriculum.[6]

ADDITIONAL BENEFITS

One additional benefit of allowing students to redo work is that such a practice offers a teacher real evidence that can be used in an attempt to assess a student's effort, whether or not effort is a part of the student's actual grade. In narrative reporting on student performance, whether or not a student chooses to redo his or her work in pursuit of excellence is certainly something worth commenting upon.

Another benefit is that redo policies may also serve to foster innovation and creativity. We want our students to take intellectual risks to try new ways of solving problems and articulating viewpoints, but if the consequences for failure are too high, they will not risk it. We want students to innovate, and we want to be able to tell them when their innovations do not work, and it is only through creating this safe space for failure that students may come up with the innovations that do work. Imagine if Steve Jobs only had one chance to get the iPhone right, if he hadn't been able to try lots of ideas first and go back to the drawing board if they didn't work. As most of the great inventors and creators throughout history would attest, failure is a necessary step toward successful innovation.

A FINAL NOTE ON STANDARDS

All of this said, it must be reiterated that it is of utmost importance that in allowing redos, teachers keep their standards high. In order for a student to truly learn to exhibit grit and resiliency, he or she must be forced to reach a certain standard before being rewarded. Under no circumstances should a student be given a higher grade just because he or she tried again. If the second try fails as well, then the grade must remain the same. If a teacher does this, far from being soft on students or giving them the easy way out, he or she is being tough on them and demanding excellence, no matter how long it takes them to achieve it. In the end, it is when we fail to maintain high expectations that we truly fail our students.

NOTES

1. Paul Tough, "What if the Secret to Success Is Failure?" *New York Times Magazine*, September 14, 2011, http://www.nytimes.com/2011/09/18/magazine/what-if-the-secret-to-success-is-failure.html?pagewanted=all; Paul Tough, *How Children Succeed: Grit, Curiosity, and the Hidden Power of Character* (New York: Houghton Mifflin Harcourt, 2012).

2. Rick Wormeli, "Redos and Retakes Done Right," *Educational Leadership* 69.3 (2011): 25.

3. Ibid., 24.

4. Ibid.

5. Ibid., 23.

6. This point is drawn out in Salman Khan's recent book *The One World Schoolhouse*. Khan makes a powerful case for mastery learning, suggesting that because students are passed on with less than proficient knowledge and skills, they have gaps in their learning that almost inevitably come back to cause problems later. Salman Khan, *The One World Schoolhouse: Education Reimagined* (London: Twelve, 2012), 83–89.

Chapter 7

Grading Behaviors and Dispositions

IS THERE A PLACE FOR BEHAVIORS AND DISPOSITIONS IN A STUDENT'S GRADES?

The opening of this book suggests that grades can reflect whatever a teacher or school wishes them to, and that the critical issues are that educators be more transparent about what these grades reflect and that these decisions support student learning rather than hinder it. That said, the subsequent chapters, through an examination of various issues have, sometimes explicitly and sometimes implicitly, argued for grading practices that attempt to reflect student skill level compared to standards. How then should behaviors and dispositions—seemingly intangible qualities such as effort, attitude, and participation—factor into the grading process?

Chapter 6 made it clear that students should not be rewarded simply for putting forth a greater effort—that, of course, assumes that the grade is meant to reflect student ability and performance, not student effort. However, this may not be the case. Teachers may wish to assess students on effort and other behaviors and dispositions, and make such assessment a part of the grade. Doing so, however, is very difficult.

DISCONNECT BETWEEN A SCHOOL'S MISSION AND WHAT A SCHOOL ASSESSES

Consider the following irony: most school mission statements include a list of character traits and habits of mind that the school wishes to see its graduates embody, while at the same time, students are generally not assessed in these areas, and little to no data is collected on them. This fundamental disconnect between what schools say they hope to achieve in their mission statements and what they assess students on and report to parents and colleges is problematic. No matter how much a school talks about its mission and tries to make it a part of the students' lives, people will tend to focus on what they believe the school really cares about—the things that it grades. A teacher can tell students all term long that he or she cares most about deep thinking, but if the teacher gives assessments that only require rote memorization, then the latter is what the students will think is most important. This disconnect between the character traits we want our students to exemplify and the academic skills that dominate reporting is particularly worth thinking about given recent research, described by Paul Tough, that suggests character strengths are more important to success than cognitive skills. [1]

Whether or not schools measure their success in fulfilling their missions is a much larger issue than the scope of this book, but suffice it to say that it is an important context for considering the grading of traits such as effort, attitude, and participation. These three are mentioned only because they seem to be the behaviors and dispositions most commonly used by teachers as a part of a student's grade. However, the list could easily be expanded to include intellectual curiosity, open-mindedness, cooperation, and so on—all of the things that schools say they value most.

QUESTIONS TO CONSIDER IF GRADING BEHAVIORS AND DISPOSITIONS

In considering how to incorporate behaviors and dispositions into a grade, a teacher is faced with the following questions:

- Should they be a part of a summative grade?
- Should they be graded separately?
- Should they be built into individual assignments?
- How will a teacher truly measure whether or not students exhibit these traits?

The last is most important, for if teachers cannot measure or gain access to concrete evidence of something—if they do not have a way to tell whether or not students are actually exhibiting these behaviors—then teachers absolutely should not grade them. Despite the fact that they may be more important than other things included in the grade, this is a powerful argument against the inclusion of these traits in a grade or on a report card.

FINDING WAYS TO MEASURE BEHAVIORS AND DISPOSITIONS

Thus, if one wishes to include these traits in a grade, the trick is finding ways to measure or assess them. Whether a teacher wants them to be a part of the summative grade or a separate grade, the fact remains that one needs to find methods of measuring these seemingly intangible traits to justify reporting on them. The data that teachers collect need not be quantitative, so perhaps *measuring* is not the best word, but one needs to observe and record, just as a scientist might observe and record the behavior of animals, and draw conclusions from these observations. That said, where quantitative data is possible, it should be used. For example, the frequency with which a student chooses to redo her work can be counted as quantitative data in support of that student's strong effort.

The first step toward measuring or recording these behaviors for the purpose of incorporating them into a grade is transparency with regard to what a teacher is looking for. It is helpful to think of any given curriculum as having three parts: (1) knowledge, (2) skills, and (3) behaviors (i.e., habits and dispositions). Hard work, positive participation, curiosity, and so on— these naturally fall under behaviors. Teachers tend to spend a great deal of time outlining the knowledge and skills required to be successful in a course, yet many say very little about this third element of the curriculum despite its importance and its dominant position in school mission statements.

So, just as teachers outline knowledge and skills, they should outline behaviors, describing and providing examples of what success looks like in these areas. The next step is to look at one's assessments. If a teacher wishes to measure effort, curiosity, open-mindedness, or leadership, do his or her assessments provide opportunities for students to display these behaviors? Do the assessments even require these behaviors for success? Just as we design and align our assessments with learning goals in terms of knowledge and skills, the same must be done with behaviors. The upshot might be that we will see fewer tests and more authentic assessments since it is very difficult to exhibit behaviors and dispositions on a test. This will be particularly true if one values these character traits more than the knowledge and skills measured by traditional tests.

It must be acknowledged that the classroom is not the only area of school life in which students may display the behaviors and dispositions that a school wishes to encourage. Even if not formally assessing them, schools should look to create such opportunities and recognize and highlight the positive behaviors of students in these areas as well.

Nevertheless, here are some examples of how teachers can collect data on positive behavior through academic assessment: as mentioned above, offering rewrites and retakes provides a way to measure effort and resiliency by allowing a teacher to keep track of how often a student chooses to go back and do more work. In order to grade participation, teachers may wish to videotape a class so they can more closely analyze the level and quality of participation of each student, which can be difficult to do while running the class. If teachers wish to measure curiosity, they can allow students to select topics of their own for assignments to see if students choose something original or just stick to what was addressed in class. If teachers wish to measure creativity, they might consider allowing students to choose alternative ways in which to show their learning, checking to see if they use innovative methods or hold tight to the traditional options. If teachers want to observe open-mindedness, they can require students to have formal debates and see how well they are able to listen to an opposing view and whether or not they are willing to concede well-made points of the opposition. If teachers want to measure collaboration, they can require their students to work in groups and have them grade each other on the various traits of a good collaborator.

This is by no means a comprehensive list, but hopefully it shows the way in which teachers can create and structure assessments to allow a window into these seemingly intangible behaviors and dispositions. The challenge for making these traits part of the grade has always been how a teacher combines his or her intuition of them with a student's performance on an assessment. The solution is making these behaviors a part of the assessment—then the students' scores or grades will already have these behaviors embedded.

Keep in mind that if one is going to attempt to assess these things, then he or she must also provide instruction on them as well. That means class time must be spent explaining, discussing, demonstrating, and practicing these behaviors.

THE IMPORTANCE OF TRANSPARENCY

If they are transparent about doing so, by all means, teachers should attempt to assess these behaviors and dispositions and incorporate them into grades— perhaps then, students will take them as seriously as the content and skills that are the focus of more traditional assessment. However, if these behaviors remain separate from particular assessments but are nonetheless observable, a teacher can combine them with performance on other assessments as a percentage of the overall grade, just as an overall grade can be broken down into percentages representing either specific assessments or specific knowledge and skills. On a standards-based report card these intangibles would simply be one of many categories. Still, one must be careful in including them separately on a report card. If there is a grade for the class and then a separate assessment of behaviors and dispositions, many parents and students may tend to look at the latter as an afterthought, regardless of how central they are to a school's mission.

A CONCERN: DOES GRADING BEHAVIORS AND DISPOSITIONS LEAD TO INAUTHENTICITY?

One concern remains to be discussed: there may be a legitimate fear that if teachers grade these traits, doing so will reduce their authenticity. A teacher wants students to be curious, so they act curious in order to earn a good grade. A teacher wants students to be open-minded and consider other points of view, so they pretend to do this in order to secure their A. This is interesting in how it highlights the uniqueness of this area of the curriculum. Cheating aside, you can't fake knowing something or exhibit a skill that is an inauthentic version of itself, but a student can feign the behaviors and dispositions that a teacher wishes to see a student possess.

There are three points to make in addressing this. The first is that the purpose of this chapter was not to suggest that these behaviors and dispositions must be a part of a student's grade, but only to outline how this could be done if a teacher wishes to do it. Thus, a teacher who has serious concerns about a lack of authenticity should not make behaviors and dispositions part of a student's grade. However, that does not mean the teacher may not teach these behaviors and create assessments that require them—he or she just doesn't have to make them part of the grade.

This leads to the second point, which is that talking about these behaviors and requiring them cannot be a bad thing, for even if they are faked at the outset, the more a student practices them, the more these traits may gradually become authentic. By becoming habits, these traits become part of a person's character. The third point is simply that teachers should be able to recognize the difference between an inauthentic display of curiosity and a genuine one, which almost makes this concern a nonissue and certainly gives the teacher a topic for an important conversation with the student. In this conversation, a teacher can make sure a student knows that these behaviors are what the teacher cares about most, and make sure the student knows that teachers can distinguish between their legitimate presence and attempts at fakery.

Ultimately, educators must remember that our values tend to be reflected in what we assess and report on. Thus, teachers must think carefully about the messages that their assessments and grades send to students and their parents. Second, teachers cannot give a grade for something unless they collect genuine data about it—be it quantitative or qualitative. Certainly, following some of the strategies outlined in this chapter will pose challenges for faculty, but they are challenges one must consider and be willing to undertake if one wishes to assess students on their behaviors and dispositions.

NOTE

1. Paul Tough, *How Children Succeed: Grit, Curiosity, and the Hidden Power of Charac-ter* (New York: Houghton Mifflin Harcourt, 2012), xi–xxiv.

Chapter 8

Grading Collaborative Work

THE PROBLEM OF GRADING COLLABORATIVE WORK

Collaboration is usually included on any list of what are commonly referred to as twenty-first-century skills. While collaboration has always been important, as the world becomes increasingly globalized and people become more easily connected through technology, it is becoming even more essential that people are able to work productively with others. Because of this fact, schools and teachers are assigning more collaborative work. However, this creates a significant problem—one that often dissuades teachers from assigning collaborative work in their classes—and this is the problem of how to grade it.

Students' progress through school individually and, hence, get their own grades that, regardless of whatever information they provide, generally reflect the work of one person. So how is a teacher supposed to translate group work into an individual grade? One may simply suggest that the grade of the group be given to every individual in the group and be averaged with the other grades. But as we will see, such a policy, while not entirely inappropriate, raises a number of issues.

GRADING COLLABORATIVE SKILL VERSUS GRADING COLLABORATIVE WORK

Before further discussion, it is first important to point out that there is a difference between grading collaborative skill and grading collaborative work. With the former, there is no problem with assigning an individual grade because you can assess each individual's ability to collaborate well with others. The grading of collaborative skill would then be treated just like the grading of any other skill, particularly the behaviors and dispositions addressed in chapter 7.

Collaborative work, on the other hand, is something produced by a group—the result of the combined effort (or lack of effort, as it may be) of multiple individuals. And this is what raises the challenges, for here one is eventually required to derive an individual grade from the work of many. Still, a further distinction can be drawn between grading the group's ability to collaborate and the work produced by the group. The former would be a grading of the process—the collective collaborative skill of the group—and the latter would be a grading of the product.

By grading only the product, one is not necessarily assessing collaboration per se, since it is possible that one or two students and not the whole group could have done the work. However, with the understanding that good collaboration will almost always improve a product, simply grading the work produced will at least somewhat reflect the ability of the group to collaborate. Still, one may choose to assess both process and product in order to give a grade that reflects both.

Deciding whether to grade process or product depends on whether or not collaborative skills are actually part of the curriculum. If one believes that collaboration is simply a way to help the students better learn the curriculum, then there is no reason to assess the process, but if collaboration is an element of the curriculum, then one must assess the process so that students are receiving feedback on this element of the curriculum.

Regardless, the important point is that one must remain aware of the distinction between grading collaborative skill and grading collaborative work. It is the latter of these that raises the most problems, and to that we now turn.

SPECIFIC CHALLENGES OF GRADING COLLABORATIVE WORK

Many teachers are reluctant to give collaborative work because of the challenges that it poses for grading. These challenges—stemming from the general problem of deriving an individual grade from something produced by a group—are the problems of what can be referred to as the "free rider" and the "anchor." Both of these lead to complaints of unfairness on the part of students. The issue of the free rider refers to students who do little to no work but are lifted up and earn a good grade thanks to the work of other students. The anchor, on the other hand, is a student who, either through a poor work ethic or simply poor skills, drags down students who might have earned a higher grade had they been doing this work individually.

In both cases, you have students earning either higher or lower grades than their individual effort and skills might suggest that they deserve. Of course, the idea that people get only and exactly what they deserve is not true in the real world, where people constantly benefit or are hindered by the work of others. While there may be ways to design collaborative assignments that minimize this tendency, it can never be completely avoided. The reason why many feel that students are getting grades that they do not deserve in this scenario, and hence that the practice is unfair, is because of a generally accepted understanding that a student's grades should reflect his or her individual skill and work. Although we should always question long-standing assumptions, this is probably a sound one since each student deserves specific feedback on his or her work and skills. Thus, a compelling case can be made that if a grade is meant to reflect an individual student's knowledge and skills, then collaborative work should not be a part of it. If one's grades are meant to reflect an individual's reading, writing, or quantitative skills, then collaborative work is a problem.

That leaves us with a conundrum: more and more teachers are assigning collaborative work, both because it has been deemed an effective way to learn and because collaboration is an increasingly valued skill; yet at the same time, it is not exactly fair to use it in determining an individual grade. Even leaving aside moral questions of fairness, using collaborative work as a part of an individual grade simply may lead to grades that are inaccurate. So what is a teacher to do?

APPROACHES TO GRADING COLLABORATIVE WORK

There are four approaches to grading collaborative work, as follows:

1. Do not grade it.
2. Grade each individual's contribution to the work separately.
3. Grade only the final product and assign the same grade to each student.
4. Give a grade that is a combination of the individual's contribution and an assessment of the final product.

Each of these methods has different implications, and we will now examine each method in turn.

Do Not Grade Collaborative Work

The simplest option is not to grade the collaborative work at all. As stated above, a strong argument can be made that grades should only reflect an individual's abilities, and hence, collaborative work should not be a part of a student's grade.

This does not mean one should not assign collaborative work. There is no reason why everything students do must be part of their grade, and hopefully work with others will tap into some internal motivation that will cause the students to work hard even if they are not being graded. A teacher may simply assign ungraded collaborative work because he or she believes the experience will help prepare the students for real life, which, after all, is the true goal of education. Furthermore, ungraded collaborative work can be used as an effective way to prepare students for individual assessments on the same material.

Grade Each Individual's Contribution to the Work

A second approach to grading collaborative work is to assign students grades based on their individual contribution to the work. This is also in keeping with the argument that an individual's grade should only reflect his or her own work. This grade could be based on the individual student's collaborative skill (if, as noted earlier, this is part of the curriculum and teachers provide instruction about the skill) or on the specific work done by the individual student.

The challenge of this method is in determining both how well each individual collaborated and what each individual contributed to the final product. In order to assess how well an individual collaborated, a teacher must be able to observe the group in action, but because the group may not always be working in the presence of the teacher, he or she may wish to have students rate other members of their group on their ability to collaborate.

Determining what each individual member contributed to the final product can be even trickier depending on the nature of the project assigned. To aid in this endeavor, the following strategies may be employed. A teacher can assign students particular roles or even particular component tasks of the larger product that can be looked at independently from one another. Each role or task can even be accompanied by its own specific rubric to be used in assessing it. The danger is that, taken to the extreme, it ends up being a series of individual tasks lumped together, rather than something produced through genuine collaboration. Of course, with genuine collaboration, it is very difficult to separate out the individual contributions. Still, there are projects in which students perform different tasks and play different roles but are aided and motivated by the encouragement and feedback of others, and this certainly qualifies as collaboration.

Although this approach might represent an acceptable compromise between not grading collaborative work and giving all students the same grade based on the final product, it does undercut the authenticity of the collaborative experience. Outside of school, groups succeed and fail as units—if the overall product is poor, it doesn't matter that one person may have done a really good job with his or her own individual task. If this is a lesson we want to teach and a situation we want students to learn to grapple with, then perhaps we should employ the next approach.

Grade the Final Product and Assign the Same Grade for Each Student

As noted, this method may open itself up to valid criticisms of unfairness and may result in individual grades that do not accurately reflect an individual's ability. However, grading collaborative work in this manner is much more authentic and does more to prepare students for the reality of life outside of school. In fact, there may be no better way to teach students the deeply important lesson that their actions affect others, and that the actions of others affect them.

Inequality, unfairness, interpersonal conflict—this is the stuff of life, the stuff that students who spend eighteen years working in isolation will be unequipped to handle. As research increasingly suggests, more may be learned from failure and setback than from success. Collaborative assignments allow our students—particularly our best students who might otherwise breeze through school having nothing but success along the way—to deal with a little adversity, but if they are given grades based only on their individual work, then the adversity essentially vanishes.

Of course, transparency is once again paramount, and if a teacher chooses to abide by this philosophy and employ this method, then he or she must make the rationale clear to the students and, probably, their parents.

Assign a Grade That Combines Individual Contribution and Final Product

If a teacher wants students to have a more authentic collaborative experience but is not willing to completely discount individual contributions to the work, then he or she may compromise by giving students a grade that is a combination of their individual work and an assessment of the final product. For example, 50 percent of a student's grade can be based on individual work and 50 percent on the overall product. Of course, these percentages can be altered depending on how a teacher feels about all of the issues raised above. Still, basing a percentage of the grade on the end product and, hence, the work or lack of work of others, keeps the practice open to the challenges of unfairness and inaccuracy. However, students and parents may be much more willing to accept it given that it is balanced by an individual grade.

In fact, balancing individual work with the final product may be the most authentic since outside of school, while people do succeed and fail as groups, a person who does good work for a failing organization may have that work recognized, resulting in individual compensation or accolades and maybe even a better job at another organization.

Other Alternatives

The above describes the four general approaches to grading collaborative work, but there are other more creative alternatives that a teacher may employ. These will all depend on the nature of the task assigned, but some possibilities are explained below.

If a collaborative assignment is a long-term project, a teacher may build individual incentives into the group work. For example, collaborative work can be assigned in which students earn points for their group based on quiz scores by group members, while the teacher keeps track of individual scores and gives bonuses for the individuals with the highest averages at the end of the project.

In projects where students do need to take on different roles, the teacher can allow them to apply for specific roles with an awareness that the more important roles give them potential to earn a higher grade—one that is still determined by the final product. For example, let's say a group is performing a skit. In this case, the director of the student performance might automatically earn a higher grade than someone who plays only a small role, with both grades remaining tied to an assessment of the final product.

A teacher may use peer assessment to gauge the value of an individual student's contributions to a project. Here's one way to do this: a teacher can assign a group a certain amount of points based on his or her assessment of the final product and then allow the students to split them up as they see fit based on their view of each individual's contribution. For example, imagine a teacher gives a project a B in a system where a B has a number equivalent of 85. There are four students in the group, so the teacher gives them 340 points (85 × 4) to split up as they see fit. They would be required to come to unanimous agreement on the allotment to ensure that students did not attempt to unfairly take advantage of one another. This method has the added bonus of requiring students to reflect on their work, discuss what they did, advocate for themselves, or face the reality of their own shortcomings and own up to them.

Schools that assign a great deal of collaborative work may even consider modifying their report cards so that students receive two grades, one for their own work and one for work done collaboratively. Such a system may reveal some interesting trends over time about how well a student works with others and whether he or she is more suited for work in isolation or in a group.

Based on all of the above, it should be clear that the grading of collaborative work is a complicated issue. While the challenges of doing so are important to consider, one should not allow the tail to wag the dog and decide against practices that are pedagogically sound and important just because they create challenges for assessment and grading policies. In the end, grading is secondary, and so long as the teacher is transparent about what a grade reflects and schools come up with policies and rationales for how and why collaborative work factors into individual student grades, then teachers should feel comfortable assigning and assessing this work. Again, the goal of grading is the same as that of education writ large—to help students learn, and if collaborative work furthers this goal, then it should be employed regardless of its impact on grades and our ability to use them to accurately sort and rank students.

Chapter 9

Self-Assessment and Self-Grading

This chapter may seem only tangentially related to the concept of grades but is actually more connected than one might think. Self-assessment obviously refers to students assessing their own work. Hence, the first part of this chapter is about helping students to self-assess accurately and about creating methods to ensure that students actually go through the process. Once we have looked at this, we will then look at the radical possibilities of having students actually give themselves grades.

Three possibilities for self-assessment are discussed: (1) self-assessment before a student hands in work, (2) self-assessment after a student has handed in work, and (3) self-assessment that actually determines the student's grade. These practices build on one another and can all be used together as a systematic and comprehensive assessment policy.

SELF-ASSESSMENT BEFORE HANDING IN WORK

The first steps toward helping students accurately self-assess their work is to give them a clear rubric for success along with specific exemplars. While rubrics may take many forms, for purposes of self-assessment, a rubric that comes in the form of a checklist, particularly a list of questions, is the most effective. As students read the rubric, they will essentially be asking questions of themselves, which is, after all, the essence of self-assessment. For example:

- Do your subjects agree with your verbs?
- Did you show all of your work?
- Did you incorporate five quotations into your essay?

   - Is the conclusion of your lab report clearly linked to the data that you
     collected?

Specific questions such as these are much more effective than simply re-
minding students to check their work. "Check it for what?" they probably
wonder.

   The above examples are yes or no questions, but certainly rubrics can
move beyond that and actually ask students to rate their own performance:

   - How convincingly do you support your thesis?
   - How accurate was your hypothesis?
   - How clear and concise are your answers?
   - How well does your project link the course material to your own experi-
     ence?

Students can be given any number of options for rating themselves. A teacher
can have students give themselves letter grades or simply ratings along the
lines of excellent, good, fair, and so on.

   Depending on how much time students have to engage in this process,
they could even explain why they gave themselves the rating that they did.
This step will have the benefit of forcing them to truly reflect on their work
rather than just check the boxes to get the self-assessment done. This type of
metacognitive analysis—not just doing their work, but thinking about the
process of doing their work—will surely help students develop as thinkers. A
teacher may also ask students to indicate how much time they spent on an
assignment or to describe their thought process in approaching the assignment. Finally, a teacher may even ask a student, "What do you think your
overall grade should be, and why?" The information provided by this policy
will give teachers much greater insight into the student's work, allowing
them to provide more specific and accurate feedback to the student.

   This works only if the students are motivated to genuinely and honestly
engage in the process. This is why teachers should require students to hand in
their self-assessment rubric along with their actual work. If the students do
not make a good-faith effort to complete the rubric, then the teacher does not
need to accept the assignment. Of course, the true incentive for a student to
genuinely engage in the self-assessment process should be the possibility of
improving the quality of his or her work. If that is not enough, the teacher can
offer other incentives to get the student to engage in the process. The simplest way of doing this would be to give a separate grade for the self-
assessment—perhaps even offering a bonus if the student's assessment of his
or her own work lines up with the teacher's.

   In an ideal world, this would lead to higher grades for everyone. After all,
if your self-assessment tells you that you are deficient in some area, why not
go back and fix it?

SELF-ASSESSMENT AFTER HANDING IN WORK

Another method of implementing self-assessment is to have students assess their own work after they have handed it in. The teacher should mark up the work, make comments on it, and give it back to the student, but should neither put a grade on it nor hand back a completed rubric. The teacher should probably complete the rubric so that he or she does not have to go through the work again, but should not share it with the student at this time.

In fact, the teacher should give the students a blank copy of the rubric along with their work and ask the students to fill it out themselves based on the feedback the teacher has provided through his or her comments. This method also allows the teacher to assess the student's ability to self-assess. A simple and powerful way to do this would be to place the rubric the teacher filled out side by side with the rubric completed by the student. The closer they match up, the better the student did at assessing his or her own work. Again, bonuses could be built in to provide the students incentive to take this self-assessment seriously.

The added benefit of this method is that it forces students to carefully read the feedback that you have given them on their work. This closer attention to feedback combined with improving self-assessment skills is bound to lead to improvement in student performance in addition to simply encouraging and developing an important life skill.

STUDENTS GRADING THEMSELVES

Once students have practice in these methods of self-assessment, then maybe they are ready to make the leap and actually assign themselves a grade that will count. Although this step sounds radical and most people assume students will just give themselves. As this author's experience suggests that this is generally not the case. First, students must be trained to self-assess in the manner described above, and second, the teacher must be willing to spend additional time monitoring the process of self-grading.

As in the previous scenario, teachers should give the students feedback without a grade (although the teacher should record one for his or her records). Then the student can assign his or her own grade and communicate this, along with a detailed rationale—either in writing or in a face-to-face conference—to the teacher. Despite students' desire for high grades, one will find that if the students have been trained properly, they assign themselves a grade fairly close to the grade the teacher would have assigned. Often, students tend to be harder on themselves than the teacher would have been, particularly during face-to-face conversations. Ideally the teacher would meet with each student, and in doing so he or she will likely find that students have a pretty hard time telling the teacher face-to-face that they are giving themselves a grade they do not deserve.

These conversations are generally wonderful opportunities for further learning, especially if the teacher allows the student to maintain control. If the student's grade is drastically inaccurate, the teacher can simply ask questions that will help the student see the work in a more accurate light, and ultimately, the student should find the appropriate grade. Often in this process, teachers will see things, for good and for bad, that they may have missed or misunderstood, which is a reason why sometimes grades determined in this manner may even be more accurate.

Obviously, it is unlikely that a teacher could go through this process on all assignments or even all major ones, but it is worth implementing even if only once in a while. It empowers students, helps them to look critically at their own work, forces them to advocate for themselves, and, best of all, they can't complain about their grades anymore.

All of these options present opportunities to enhance student learning. They help to give students a better sense of the teacher's expectations and about the quality of their own work. They encourage focused self-reflection combined with the motivation to take concrete steps toward improvement. They bring students into the grading process as more equal participants, making the grading of assessments less adversarial. This makes students feel less like grading is about judgments coming down from on high and more about conversations between two people about the quality of someone's work.

Chapter 10

Technology and the Grading Process

In this chapter we turn to the impact of technology on the grading process. Given the rapid pace of change, one must write about technology with caution, since ideas may quickly become outdated or obsolete. With that in mind, this chapter says very little about specific technological tools, but rather makes a more general point about the underlying goals in using any technology in the grading process. If one of the fundamental purposes of grading is to provide feedback for students that is useful for growth, then what we need to look at are ways in which technology can help us do this better.

TOWARD THE CONCEPT OF *ASSIDERE*

The verb *assess*—which is what we are doing when grading student work—comes from the Latin *assidere*, which means "to sit next to."[1] Based on this, one may argue that the best way to truly assess a student's abilities is to sit next to that student in order to, as closely as possible, monitor his or her progress. Perhaps in an ideal world this is how grading would happen—a teacher would sit next to each student and engage in dialogue over his or her work. Obviously, with student-to-teacher ratios as they are, such a situation is impossible. However, through the use of technology, teachers can create situations that attempt to simulate the experience of a teacher sitting next to a student.

For example, when using a tool such as a shared online document, if a teacher writes a comment on a student's work, the student receives that comment via e-mail (as well as on the document) and then can respond to that comment, prompting an e-mail to the teacher. This type of dialogue is much more similar to a teacher and student sitting next to one another than traditional comments that are given to a student with little potential for dialogue.

With more and more software that can record audio, teachers and students can embed voice comments on a student's work so that, while not sitting next to one another, they are literally speaking to one another. Of course, the next step would be a video recording to even further personalize the process. Furthermore, with software that allows people to voice record over images, one can imagine teachers recording themselves as they go through the process of assessing a student's work. The teacher could be circling and commenting upon things just as if he or she were sitting next to the student going over the student's work. This would make the grading process extremely transparent and likely much more effective in promoting student growth.

Speaking of process, another advantage to using a program such as a shared online document is that a teacher, through access to the revision history, can actually look back at the process a student undertook in completing the work. This also creates a situation similar to a teacher sitting next to the student as he or she is working.

It is likely that the tools will only get better, making it easier and easier for a teacher to implement *assidere*—to assess students' work in the original sense of the word, as if sitting next to them. This will undoubtedly enhance student learning.

TECHNOLOGY AND ELECTRONIC PORTFOLIOS

Another way technology can make the grading process more conducive to student learning is through the ease with which it allows students to assemble a portfolio of their work that is constantly accessible to both teacher and student. Hard copies of work that were turned in and handed back are easily lost. A grade and some notes may be recorded, but the work is unlikely to ever be referred to or looked at again.

Now students can have electronic folders that hold all of their work and that are shared with their teachers. This allows the teacher to do a much better job of tracking the student's progress with real examples and not just grades. This can be very helpful in allowing a teacher to identify persistent problems that need to be addressed and specific improvements that have been made. Both are important to point out to students, and certainly when meeting with a student, the ability to instantly view any piece of a student's work can make for an extremely effective conference.

In terms of giving summative grades, the existence of a digital portfolio allows a teacher to more accurately assess the student's work as a whole, and being able to do this at the end of the term might result in a more accurate grade than the average of assessments of individual pieces of work. Teachers certainly do not have time to regularly look at work more than once, but at least an accessible portfolio allows for this possibility.

Digital portfolios also allow students to treat their assignments as work in progress. Teachers who are more concerned with what students *can do* than with when work *is due* can allow students virtually unlimited opportunities to improve all of their assignments. In some programs, teacher feedback is instantaneously available to a student, and then the teacher is alerted if a student has made a change to his or her work. Or if students simply stumble upon an idea that they think would improve some work that they had done earlier in the term, they can go back and change the work accordingly, and the teacher will be alerted.

This essentially allows for an asynchronous, but constant, process of re-writes and redos. If this is something teachers are in favor of, then digital portfolios only aid teachers in grading by allowing them to see the revision history, making them aware of exactly what the students added, what they deleted, and what they changed. As mentioned earlier, teachers who often preach the importance of process will also enjoy this feature of shared online documents since it allows teachers a window into the process, one through which they can view every stage of a student's work, not to mention how much time a student put in and when he or she actually did the work.

Last, digital portfolios serve a nonpedagogical purpose that is, nonetheless, very useful to teachers. It allows them to offer evidence to anyone— student, parent, administrator—at any time for why they assigned the grade that they did.

THE POTENTIAL FOR A SHORTER FEEDBACK LOOP

Generally, the shorter the feedback loop, the more likely a student is to learn from the feedback provided by a teacher, and using technology to assess a student's work can allow that student to receive a teacher's feedback in a much more timely fashion.

Because comments on a shared online document come in real time and students are alerted to them via e-mail, they have instant access to the teacher's feedback. They do not even have to wait until a teacher hands their work back to see what the teacher thought of it. Furthermore, a student can respond to a comment as soon as a teacher posts it, again, as if they were sitting next to one another. No longer will a student have to wait for the teacher to finish all of the grading before getting his or her own work back. This means students will receive feedback quickly, and any dialogue between teacher and student is more likely to occur when the work is fresher in both of their minds.

This is not to say that technology necessarily makes the grading process quicker, but at the very least, some students will get their work back sooner since they will not have to wait until all work is assessed. Teachers can have a system for whose work they begin with so that each student has equal opportunity to get work back more quickly over the course of the year.

Another element of shortening the feedback loop is how quickly teachers can see student work. With a digital portfolio, a teacher can take a look at student homework before a class even begins. Rather than looking at the homework after class and realizing the students really had trouble with something that could have been addressed during class, the teacher can go into class with an awareness of where students had difficulty and address it immediately.

This chapter has pointed out ways in which technology can enhance the grading process for teachers and students. However, the goal is to support student learning, not simply to utilize technology, so one should always reflect on whether or not the use of technology is furthering that goal. If students feel that they learn more from feedback written by hand on hard copies of their work, then that is what a teacher should do. It is likely that different students will prefer feedback in different ways, and thus it is worth a teacher's time to survey students and find out how each one prefers to get feedback and then differentiate accordingly. Technology can be a tool for learning, but it is the learning that matters, not the tools themselves, so if other tools work better for certain students then a teacher must use those tools, whether low-, high-, or no-tech.

NOTE

1. Grant Wiggins, "A True Test: Toward a More Authentic and Equitable Assessment," *Phi Delta Kappan* 70.9 (1989): 708.

Chapter 11

The Issue of Inconsistency

THE PROBLEM

This chapter addresses the very large challenge of trying to gain consistency in grading at the levels of individual teachers, academic departments, schools, districts, states, and perhaps even the nation. This chapter also examines the question of whether or not inconsistency is actually a problem that should concern educators. Regardless, aiming for consistency of grading at any level is a very tall order given the seeming impossibility of getting so many teachers to apply the same standards—standards that are often subjective—to their assessment of student work.

In a chapter titled "The Future of Transcripts" in Salman Khan's book *The One World Schoolhouse*, he goes right at the question of how society "settle[s] the question of which academic or personal criteria really matter as predictors of success."[1] Addressing colleges and employers, Khan asks, "in the name of fairness and also practicality, how can you be confident that you're comparing apples to apples?"[2] Khan is very much concerned with social and economic inequality and its effect on student work, but he also finds problems with the entire notion of using grades to compare students:

> How do conventional schools appraise their students? The first way, of course, is by letter grades. Could anything be less precise, less meaningful, or more capricious? As everybody knows, all schools have "easy markers" and "hard markers." If standards can vary widely on either side of a hallway or a row of lockers, how much less uniform will they be from state to state or nation to nation? Yet letter grades are where the rankings start. . . . If the individual grades are hazy and subjective, why should we imagine that their composite is precise and scientific? GPA is at best a blunt instrument. True it can provide a general idea of whether a kid showed up, engaged with school, and played the

game. But it is sheer blindness and folly to imagine that GPA alone tells you much about a student's intelligence or creativity. Does someone with a 3.6 necessarily have more to offer to the world than someone with a 3.2? I wouldn't bet on it.[3]

Khan's point is twofold. First he articulates the fact that grades may tell us very little about a student's potential for success outside of school. Khan is certainly correct on this point when grades have not been clearly defined, as is often the case. However, if grades are clearly defined, then they may be able to provide reliable information about a student's ability. Of course, whether or not these abilities are transferable to the world beyond school depends on the nature of the assessment tasks given to students. Being a good test taker may tell us very little about real-world potential; being a creative thinker and an innovative problem solver may tell us a lot.

More relevant to the topic of this chapter is Khan's second point. Here he argues not that grades are not good predictors of student potential per se, but that, due to their arbitrariness, they are not good predictors of student potential relative to other students. Given the perceived high stakes of the college admissions process and the genuine high stakes of the job market, this inconsistency would seem to be a significant issue. Thus, addressing this problem is important for many people.

Still, as stated many times already, the purpose of grades should not be to sort and rank students, which implies that teachers should be less concerned with whether or not grading effectively achieves those purposes and should spend more time worrying about whether or not grading supports further learning. That said, treating students fairly in the implementation of any facet of the educational process should be of utmost concern to all teachers. Thus, even though sorting and ranking are not our concern, the unfairness involved must be addressed, particularly since this unfairness affects not only students' lives beyond school, but also their learning while in school.

There are two ways in which this unfairness can negatively affect student learning. The first, which applies only to high school and college, deals with student decision making when choosing classes. If a certain teacher is thought to be a more difficult grader, students are less likely to enroll in that person's class, regardless of what they know about the quality of the teacher and the education that he or she provides. It is not uncommon to hear a student say, "Mrs. X is supposed to be awesome, but she's a really hard grader, so I'm not taking her class because it will kill my GPA." Clearly, making decisions about which classes to take based on their perceptions of how the teacher grades rather than the learning that may occur may have a negative impact on that students' education.

The second negative impact of inconsistent grading is that students may have difficulty gaining an accurate picture of their own skills. If a student earns an A in a class where the same work would have earned a B with another teacher, or if a student earns a B one year and then an A the next, not because his or her work has improved but because the grading is different, the student will be very much misled in the understanding of his or her skills and performance. Whether the student truly deserved an A or a B remains to be seen, but the point is that if one of the critical purposes of grades is to provide students with feedback, then inconsistent and inevitably inaccurate feedback does not help the cause.

Having now examined the problem, let us turn to ways not necessarily of solving it, but at least of minimizing it.

METHODS OF MINIMIZING INCONSISTENCY

There are a number of reasons why we will always have to live with a degree of inconsistency. The sheer number of teachers is perhaps the most obvious. Yet, even at the level of individual schools that may not have that many teachers, the fact of the matter is that teachers are often grading things that are subjective, which makes judgments almost inherently inconsistent. If all assessments were standardized tests, this would not be the issue—hence the term *standardized*. However, educators increasingly believe that little is gained from standardized tests. Yes, they can provide certain information about a student, but neither preparing students for them nor the act of students taking them hold much educational value.

On the other hand, projects, presentations, performances, and essays, which may give us information about more important skills than an objective test, and which serve as learning exercises in and of themselves, are much more subjective, and hence, more difficult to grade consistently. It is relatively easy to objectively measure someone's knowledge, more difficult to measure someone's skills, and even more difficult to measure positive behaviors and dispositions—which are perhaps the most important things our students can develop. As teachers begin to use more authentic, open-ended, and creative assessments, the ability to measure student performance consistently diminishes, and we are left to think about how we can minimize, not eliminate, inconsistency.

The first step is for schools to define what each grade they give means in terms of a general standard of performance. Once this is done, departments can then take those standards and apply specifics to them that are more explicit in addressing actual elements of the curriculum. These standards can then be even further parsed out to apply to specific courses, taking into account the increased expectations as students progress through their course of study.

This sets the framework for more consistent grades, and then, at the level of an individual course, there are five things that a team of teachers can do to minimize inconsistency:

1. Give common assessments that have been generated collaboratively among the teachers.
2. Use common rubrics, also generated collaboratively, that have clear and accurate descriptors of the various levels of performance in the various categories being assessed.
3. Collect or collaboratively generate exemplars of work corresponding to the various levels of performance.
4. Grade and discuss student work together.
5. Continually revisit this process in order to update and fine-tune the rubrics and exemplars.

We will now explore each one of these in turn.

Giving students common assessments is an absolutely necessary first step. One cannot expect consistent grading between two sections of a class if the students take different tests and do different projects. It is very difficult to say that an A means the same thing for two students who had to do entirely different things to earn it. This is not to say that common assessments need to be identical, just that teachers agree that they are requiring the same knowledge and skills. One English teacher can ask students to compare and contrast two characters from a novel and another one can ask students to compare and contrast two symbols in a short story, but at the end of the day, the standards for these assessments can be the same, and hence, one may consider this a common assessment.

This example makes clear why it is so important that these assessments are generated collaboratively by a team of teachers. This allows teachers to personalize assignments while working with other teachers teaching the same course to ensure that the assessment still achieves the same goals. While this means assignments might be slightly different, this may be preferable to a situation in which one teacher makes the assessment and the others administer it.

Once these common assessments have been designed, teachers must turn to the task of designing rubrics that have clear and accurate descriptors of the various levels of performance in the various categories being assessed. This will undoubtedly be even more arduous than actually designing the assessments themselves, but is a critical step to minimizing inconsistency in grading. It will be particularly important how teachers decide to phrase the descriptors, since this information, in addition to being important to the student, will also serve as a handy reference tool to the teacher—one that he or she can easily apply to the particular work that is being assessed.

After rubrics have been designed, the next step is to provide exemplars. Rubrics provide general descriptors; exemplars—as the term indicates—provide specific examples of various levels of performance. This may be even more critical to minimizing inconsistency in grading because, while it can be very easy for teachers to agree that a student's evidence must be clear, specific, and persuasive, it is a lot more challenging to get those teachers to agree on what clear, specific, and persuasive evidence looks like. Ideally, teachers would find examples for every level of performance for every category on the rubric. Going through this exercise is time consuming, but it can be powerful for teachers, and if done properly will result in much more consistent grades—and probably better instruction.

Once the teachers have explained the rubric to their students, discussed the various exemplars with them, and administered the assessment, they should grade some student work together until they come to agreement on what the grade should be. Coming to consensus may be difficult, but it must be done if one wishes to reduce inconsistency. Having a clear rubric is very helpful since teachers should constantly refer back to it, applying only the standards articulated in the rubric to the work in question.

This step may require teachers to amend their rubric, and there is nothing wrong with that. In fact, that is why step 5 is to continually revisit and update the rubrics and exemplars. It is difficult to find the perfect rubric for any assignment, and one should always enter this entire process aware that it must be one of perpetual improvement. Periodically, teachers should get together to grade student work in this manner. It may be helpful for them to each bring work that they have already graded and allow other teachers to grade it without knowledge of what grade the original teacher has assigned to it. If teachers are generally giving the same grades, then that is the evidence that the grades are relatively consistent. If not, then it is time to have further discussion and likely to go back and refine the rubrics and exemplars.

The above represents an effective strategy for gaining consistency in grades at a school level; however, once one widens the scope, things get more difficult. School districts could attempt to (and probably do) mandate standards that teachers are supposed to use when grading. However, when these standards are not established by the people actually working in a school, they will be less effective. Gaining consistency in grading must be a collaborative process and, hence, standards cannot be mandated from the outside. Even if one tried to implement a similar system on a wider scale, the sheer increase in numbers would undoubtedly lead to greater statistical inconsistency—which is of course why it seems completely ludicrous to compare the grades of students across the country from all sorts of different schools. Inconsistent grading is inevitable, and while we should try to minimize it, perhaps the question we should be asking is simply how to deal with its existence.

HOW TO DEAL WITH THE INEVITABILITY OF INCONSISTENCY

Perhaps one of the best strategies in dealing with inconsistency is to de-emphasize grades to begin with. If educators focus more on actual learning than on grades, then the inconsistency of grades matters a great deal less. As long as students are receiving feedback that helps them continue to learn, the way in which that feedback is labeled or averaged is less relevant. Parents reading this may be thinking that inconsistency matters a great deal since college acceptances are determined by grades and, hence, that inconsistency is deeply unfair. But grading should be more about helping students learn and less about ranking or sorting them. If schools develop systems of grading more focused on learning and less easily quantifiable than the current systems, colleges will have to find other ways to sort and rank their applicants.

NOTES

1. Salman Khan, *The One World Schoolhouse: Education Reimagined* (London: Twelve, 2012), 214.
2. Ibid.
3. Ibid.

Chapter 12

The Advantages and Disadvantages of Using Rubrics

To most educators the advantages of rubrics are obvious, and in a large majority of schools, their use is accepted as best practice. However, there are those who still hold out and do not see the value of using rubrics to assist in grading student work. This chapter attempts to clearly lay out the advantages of using rubrics but also looks at potential drawbacks. While most of the arguments in this book, either explicitly or implicitly, support the use of rubrics in grading, one should take seriously the potential disadvantages and allow them to inform one's use of rubrics in order to maximize the advantages for both teachers and students.

ADVANTAGE 1: RUBRICS ENCOURAGE CONSISTENCY

Chapter 11 went into great detail on how rubrics help to achieve consistency in grading, so there is little reason to spend much time on this point here. Suffice it to say that a detailed rubric, one that clearly defines different standards of performance, will help to ensure that the same standards are applied to student work. This is true not only between different teachers using the same rubric, but even of the individual teacher. The time of day, the mood you are in, the number of items you have already graded, your general knowledge of the student whose work is being graded—all of these things can affect an individual teacher's perception of student work and can result in inconsistencies in grading. Using a rubric will not entirely solve this problem, but it will go a long way toward minimizing it by serving as a constant reminder to the teacher of exactly which standards he or she is supposed to be applying to the work.

ADVANTAGE 2: RUBRICS PROVIDE CLEAR EXPECTATIONS

The second advantage to the use of rubrics is that they are very helpful to a teacher in making his or her expectations for student work clear to the students. In order to gain this advantage a teacher must be sure that students have copies of the rubric that will be used to grade their work well ahead of time. Particularly when combined with specific exemplars of the various levels of performance, the use of rubrics can be a very powerful tool toward raising student achievement and helping students produce better work. As noted in a previous chapter, through the clear expectations provided, rubrics can also serve as effective devices in helping students learn to self-assess their work. This, in turn, leads to further improvements in performance, not to mention the fact that self-assessment is an important life skill that will help students in all future endeavors.

ADVANTAGE 3: RUBRICS OFFER USEFUL FEEDBACK

Much earlier in the book it was made clear that one of the primary purposes for using grades is to provide students with feedback, and that this feedback must be useful in helping students to improve their work. The use of rubrics in grading is an effective way to ensure that the feedback that a teacher provides is useful to students. Certainly, general comments on a student's work can be useful, but the clarity with which a rubric can provide feedback on different standards of performance in different skill areas can be a tremendous asset to student growth. A well-designed rubric gives students a clear visual representation (along with written descriptors) of how they performed—in what areas they excelled and in what areas they need to improve. Yes, these things may be captured in a teacher's comments, but they will not be as clearly laid out as they can be on a rubric.

ADVANTAGE 4: RUBRICS ALLOW PROGRESS TO BE MORE EASILY TRACKED

The clarity of the layout of a rubric also makes it much easier for students and teachers to track progress. This is particularly so if a class is focused on developing specific skills to which the same rubric can be applied over the course of the year. Again, the visual layout is an advantage here because students can simply see how they are progressing up a scale in the various categories addressed by the rubric. This makes it easier to get students to adopt the idea that their goal should be to improve, not simply to earn a certain grade. In contrast to general written comments, students can place two consecutive rubrics next to one another and very clearly see the areas in which they are making progress and the areas in which they are stagnant. Again, this visual representation allows the students to focus on their progress, and not on the grade at the bottom.

The ease with which rubrics allow progress to be tracked is also a great advantage to the teacher who can more clearly ascertain student strengths and weaknesses with a glance at a series of rubrics. Without this, he or she would either be trying to remember all of this information as it pertains to each student or would have to go back and read previous comments to find the information needed. Having this information easily discernible and accessible is very helpful for a teacher when writing term-ending comments or during conferences with students and parents. If the teacher is better able to communicate an accurate picture of a student's performance in comments and conferences, this will be a step toward further growth on the part of the student.

ADVANTAGE 5: RUBRICS CLARIFY THE LINK BETWEEN THE QUALITY OF WORK AND THE GRADE

Perhaps the most important advantage to using a rubric is the way in which it can clearly indicate the link between the grade given and the quality of the student's work. Many of the sections above speak to the clarity with which rubrics present their information, and the overall impact of this is that it becomes less likely that students will see the grade at the bottom as some mysterious judgment the teacher has placed upon their work, and more likely that the student will view the grade as a clear result of the level of work that has been done.

ADVANTAGE 6: RUBRICS ALLOW TEACHERS TO GRADE MORE EFFICIENTLY

From a teacher's perspective, the best advantage of using rubrics may be that they help you get your grading done more quickly. While this certainly might be the case, there is a pedagogical benefit to the efficiency as well, which is that the feedback loop is shortened, allowing students to receive this feedback when their own work is fresher in their minds. This is a critical component of making sure that feedback is useful for student improvement.

It would seem from the above that rubrics are an overwhelmingly positive tool for teachers to use in their quest to help students learn as much as possible. But there may be some not-so-obvious drawbacks, and to those we will now turn.

DISADVANTAGE 1: RUBRICS PLACE LIMITS ON STUDENTS

One of the advantages cited above is the clear expectations that rubrics give students. However, one might argue that these expectations actually put restrictions on students and limit their ability to see new and different ways of doing things. This may only be exacerbated when rubrics are accompanied by exemplars and students have models for what various standards of performance on an assignment look like. This may discourage students from truly thinking for themselves and coming up with new and innovative methods for completing a certain task. Instead, students may just do what the rubric says they should do, which might make them good at following directions, but not necessarily at being creative, original thinkers. In short, detailed and specific rubrics can take even open-ended assignments and lead to conformity, limiting not only what is required but also what can be expected of a student.

DISADVANTAGE 2: RUBRICS PLACE LIMITS ON TEACHERS

Not only might the use of rubrics in grading be limiting to the student, but a teacher might find them limiting as well. The options teachers are given to select from may not quite fit the teacher's assessment of the work. For example, imagine a rubric for an essay that uses the standards in Table 12.1 to assess a student's thesis statement.

Table 12.1

Does Not Yet Meet Expectations	Meets Expectations	Exceeds Expectations
Your thesis statement lacks clarity and focus, and does not reflect original thinking about the topic.	Your thesis statement is clear, but it could be more focused or reflect more original thinking about the topic.	Your thesis statement is focused, clear, and reflects deeply original thinking about the topic.

On its face, this seems like a useful rubric, but what does a teacher do if a student's thesis statement seems to reflect deeply original thinking, but it lacks clarity and focus? There is no box that applies. Does the teacher circle the part that says, "reflects deeply original thinking" and the part that says, "your thesis lacks clarity and focus"? If so, what message is being sent to the student? Did he exceed expectations? Has he not met expectations yet? Or should he simply split the difference and assume that he met expectations but did not exceed them? None of these would be correct, but they would, none-theless, be the messages sent due to the limitations of the rubric.

That is how a rubric can be limiting for a teacher relative to specific categories, but it can also be limiting in a larger sense, for rubrics can make it difficult for a teacher to provide a holistic assessment of a student's work. This leads to the following disadvantage of using rubrics.

DISADVANTAGE 3: WHOLES ARE NOT NECESSARILY EQUAL TO THE SUM OF THEIR PARTS

A rubric breaks the assessment down into various skills, components, or criteria, and the student is rated in each of these areas. From this series of ratings, a teacher generally determines an overall grade for the assignment. This grade may be an average of the scores in the various categories, or each category may be weighted and then added together. Whatever the method, individual ratings in different areas are combined to establish an overall grade. The grade the rubric spits out may seems lower than the teacher's general sense of what the work as a whole deserves. And of course, it could just as easily be the other way around. One could add up the ratings in various sections and end up with a higher grade than the work seems to deserve. In either case, rubrics can lead to a grade that, to the teacher, just doesn't seem right.

DISADVANTAGE 4: RUBRICS DECREASE THE ABILITY OF TEACHERS TO GRADE EFFICIENTLY

The final potential disadvantage of rubrics may strike the reader as odd, since Advantage 6 was about increased efficiency. However, one can make the case that filling out a rubric is more time intensive, particularly if the teacher is putting comments on the student work in addition to filling out the rubric. Thus, using a rubric can seem to add to the grading process—creating paper-work to be filled out after the teacher has gone through the student's work, when it might be quicker to just write a few comments down and slap a grade on it. If this is true, then using a rubric would lengthen rather than shorten the feedback loop, which would be a detriment to student learning.

ADDRESSING POTENTIAL DRAWBACKS AND USING RUBRICS EFFECTIVELY

Despite these potential disadvantages, the reasons in favor of the use of rubrics seem stronger. However, these disadvantages must be taken into account and addressed in order to use rubrics as effectively as possible.

First, one must be careful when designing a rubric to make sure that it is not limiting to either student or teacher. To do so, a teacher must make sure that descriptors are general enough so that they can fit many different examples of student work. A rubric need not be a specific checklist of things a student must do, but rather can be composed of open-ended criteria for different levels of achievement. Really, it is the use of exemplars that can be limiting to students, so one must make certain that students are shown a range of different possibilities for excellence and are clearly told that their job is not to copy the model but to see it merely as one example of a certain standard of performance.

A teacher should feel free to circle more than one box for a given category. While this may make it difficult to determine a grade for that section, one does not necessarily have to do that. Perhaps a more enlightened rubric does not require that every element be tied to a specific grade. One may even imagine a different type of rubric that is not a list of different standards of achievement in certain categories, each with its own descriptor, but a list of statements from which a teacher circles all that are appropriate. This does not give students a clear sense of an overall performance rating, but it does give very specific feedback on what they did and did not do well.

Another way to make the rubric less limiting is to leave space for comments in each category so the teacher can add specifics or qualifying remarks when necessary. One can even imagine a rubric with a column of skills on the left and a row of levels of performance across the top, with empty boxes for the teacher to fill in specifics. In this manner, the teacher can give different reasons for different students as to why their performance in a certain area may have earned a certain rating.

Furthermore, there are two ways to approach the tension between grades for each category and the overall grade. The first is to grade each category, but not give an overall grade. These may inevitably get averaged in the grade book, but by not actually combining them into one grade on the rubric, a teacher makes it clear to students that he or she would rather have them pay attention to the specifics of what they did or did not do than the overall grade.

The second way of dealing with this tension is not to give specific grades or ratings for each category, but simply to give an overall grade that may be informed but is not determined by the performance in individual areas. This allows the teacher to assign a grade that aligns with his or her holistic impression of the work.

This may be an effective method, but one should be a little suspicious of the notion that a teacher's holistic impression may result in a more accurate grade than what the rubric suggests. What we call a holistic assessment may actually be a hazy impression—amounting to more of a gut response than anything else. While they cannot entirely be discounted, gut responses may be what lead to inconsistent grading, and, furthermore, do little in the way of providing students with specific and useful feedback on their work. A rubric takes the gut out of things and makes sure that the grade is based on specific criteria and evidence of whether or not those criteria have been met.

Regardless, it is always a good idea for teachers to give general comments at the end of a rubric. It is there that they can add what the rubric could not capture and provide a holistic assessment in addition to the more specific feedback provided by the rubric.

As to the question of efficiency, because the feedback loop is so critical to student learning, teachers should weigh how quickly certain methods of grading allow them to get work back to students with the amount and specificity of feedback that they provide. Teachers may find a different rubric or system that allows them to maximize efficiency, and that is what they should do, so long as they are not sacrificing the specificity and usefulness of the feedback that they are providing.

The final and perhaps most important factor in determining whether to use a rubric and what type of rubric one should use is the preference of the students. As stated in chapter 10, the purpose of grading is to enhance student learning, and hence, we should grade with methods and tools that benefit students. Education is about the students and not the teachers, so we should honor their preferences in terms of the type of feedback that we give them and the format of its presentation.

Chapter 13

How to Report Grades

Now that we have considered a number of issues pertaining to how grades are determined, in the final chapter of part 2, we turn to how grades are reported. To this end, three questions should be considered: What should be reported? To whom should the information be reported? When should the information be reported?

As an initial step in addressing these questions, one should first go back to the ideas in chapter 2, which detailed the following three potential purposes for grades, and one must consider how the reporting of grades advances these three purposes:

1. To generate data upon which to base decisions
2. To motivate students
3. To provide students with feedback on their work

Thus, one should think about how the reporting of grades will affect the decisions that are informed by the grades. Then one should turn to how the reporting of grades can motivate students, with an eye toward generating deep and lasting intrinsic motivation. Last, one must consider how the reporting of grades can best give students feedback that is relevant, specific, and useful. With those three issues in mind, one may then turn to the specifics of what, to whom, and when to report.

WHAT TO REPORT

In order to answer the question of what should be reported, one also needs to refer back to chapter 1. One should look at table 13.1 and select a definition that fits the template:

A grade is a/an _____ of _____ relative to _____ .

Table 13.1

Type of Information	Topic of Information	Context for Information
A grade is a/an . . .	*of . . .*	*relative to . . .*
Quantification	A student's learning	A standard
Symbol	A student's skill level at a certain time	A student's peers within a class, school, grade, or age level in a particular region
Description	A student's average skill level over a period of time	A student's starting point
Evaluation	A student's performance on an individual assessment task	All other possible outcomes
Ranking	A student's performance on a number of assessment tasks	
	A student's progress over a certain period of time	

This is the first step toward determining what is being reported, but teachers still need to work out the specifics of the form of the grade and what data will actually be included or used in determining it. Generally, grades reported will be summative in nature, so here it is worth referring back to chapter 5. This chapter should provide all of the detail that you need to make decisions about how to calculate or what to include in a grade that will serve as a summation of whatever you have decided your grade will represent.

However, it is very important to understand that one need not limit one's thinking about what should be reported to a single summative grade either for each class or as a combined GPA. Standards-based grading suggests grading students on particular standards or skills rather than individual assignments. The upshot of this is that students see multiple grades for each assignment, as opposed to a less meaningful (due to its lack of specificity) overall grade for an assignment. This concept is easily transferable to a report card, on which students might benefit from multiple grades—grades specific to the learning objectives as opposed to one grade for each class or content area. Thus, a report card might average grades in particular skill areas as opposed to particular assignments, reporting a grade for each student on each skill that was assessed. These might be organized by skills in each individual class, or, even more holistically, they might take skills across disciplines and give students a grade for a skill such as reading, which could be determined by the level of reading demonstrated in all of their classes. This method becomes more attractive if classes become more interdisciplinary and arbitrary walls between academic disciplines are broken down.

As pointed out in chapter 5, even the tradition of averaging grades is one that should be considered carefully. Teachers should consider the possibility of giving weight to a student's most recent performances, since they provide the most detail about current skill level, rather than past skill level. Still, there are alternatives to any type of summative grade, whether for a class or a standard. Teachers may consider simply reporting a list of grades representing student performance on all major assessments.

Another issue that must be considered when thinking about what to report is whether or not to report on behaviors and dispositions such as effort, attitude, and participation. As stated in chapter 7, the most important point about incorporating these traits into a grade is being transparent about doing so. If these behaviors and dispositions are part of a summative grade for a class, then it must be made clear that the grade represents more than the student's skill level in certain areas. This is why many schools have chosen to report on these traits separately, giving a summative grade for a course and then grades for other behaviors and dispositions that the school believes to be important. If one is using standards-based grades, then these traits simply become another in a list of specific areas in which a student is graded.

It is worth noting that grades on specific skills or standards and various behaviors and dispositions can be combined with a summative grade if a school feels the need to supply such a grade, whether for its own purposes or to facilitate the ease of judgments made about their students by external constituencies. Nevertheless, anytime a student's performance is boiled down to a single number, letter, or symbol, a great deal of important information is lost.

In addition to the reporting of a grade, it is relatively common for grades to be accompanied by comments written by teachers. Because writing these comments is a time-intensive process, the length and specificity of comments depends on the workloads that teachers carry in terms of number of classes, and more importantly, the total number of students. Thus, in many schools, where teachers may have upward of 100 students, comment writing—in a meaningful way that is timely and detailed—is simply not feasible. However, a number of schools are fortunate enough to be able to engage in this process, and at these places, it has the potential to be quite valuable.

Some schools give comments at the same time that grades are reported, and others give them at different times. Because of the prevalence of student and parental obsession with grades, one must think carefully about whether or not to provide grades and comments at the same time, for just as students are likely to look only at a grade on an assignment and not the teacher's comments, the same tendency may be true of students and parents when it comes to report cards. If comments come out at the same time as grades, they might be viewed as secondary, but if they come out separately, they might not be viewed at all.

Still, it seems that in most cases grades and comments should come out at the same time. While there is always a chance that comments will be overlooked, it is critical that grades, especially if they are coming in the form of a summative letter, number, or symbol, be placed in some context; some narrative must be provided if that grade is to have any meaning at all, particularly if it is to give students feedback that will encourage further learning. Therefore, if comments come out at the same time as grades, schools should do everything in their power with regard to the format of the report card to put the focus on the comment and make the grade itself appear secondary.

Of course, there are effective methods for using comments separately from grades that can actually shift the focus from the grade to the learning. One example is giving only comments at the midterm. They would provide specific feedback about what a student has done well and what he or she needs to work on. Because of the information that would be provided, this policy would have potential to do more than any number, letter, or symbol to help students improve before the term ends. If students and parents know that all they will get during a term is a narrative comment, then they will certainly pay attention to it. The more students get used to judging their own performance based on the comments that they receive, rather than the grades, the more they will be become focused on the actual learning and not just the number or letter.

Hopefully the above has provided some insight on what to report and the implications of reporting different things, and if there is one idea that is critical, it is that schools should report more than just summative numbers, letters, or symbols if they wish to provide students and their parents with meaningful feedback.

TO WHOM TO REPORT

To whom to report is a somewhat simpler question, but it has multiple dimensions since different constituencies may require different information for different purposes. Thus, we must actually combine this question with the previous one and consider what to report to whom, opening up the possibility that different information may go to different people. Below are the possible audiences for the reporting of grades:

- Students
- Parents
- Administrators
- Policymakers
- Colleges
- Employers

If the fundamental purpose of grading is to further student learning, then obviously, grades and accompanying information must be reported to students and, generally, to their parents as well. However, if we wish students to become increasingly independent, then we must be careful about exactly how much and how often parents are reported to, so as not to create a situation in which they are micromanaging their children's education.

Administrators and policymakers can also make use of information from grades, but they need not get the specifics regarding individual grades or the comments that accompany them. For the purposes of decision making regarding such things as teacher evaluation, curriculum, and overall student performance, summative grades that are more easily quantifiable actually may be more appropriate. It is important that this information be made available when needed, since this can actually help make decisions that will impact learning.

In terms of the final two constituencies—colleges and employers—as stated many times, educators should not concern themselves with working in service of these groups since the ease with which they are able to select students has little effect on student learning. That said, whatever information is given to students may also be made available to colleges and employers. However, making information useful to them should not at all be a priority for, nor an impediment to, creating systems of grading that more effectively support student learning.

However, it is worth considering multiple reporting systems so that colleges and employers get not different information, but information in a different form than students or parents. This is particularly relevant at schools whose students regularly attend highly selective colleges, and where grades have risen to the point where the range of grades is tremendously compressed. The reason for this compression is not always because performance and skills are going up, and may sometimes be related to the pervasive notion that giving low grades can destroy a student's chance of getting accepted at an ultraselective college. For this reason, schools may wish to consider separate internal and external reporting systems.

Such a two-pronged approach to grading allows a school to say to external constituencies, "yes, most of our students are very strong, and relative to their peers across the country they deserve high grades" (i.e., almost all As and Bs in the traditional paradigm), while at the same time giving students more specific and useful measures of their performance internally. While many student and parents today are not satisfied with Bs—a shock to people who went to school in previous generations—the traditional understanding of grading scales persists, so that students who average in the low-B range at strong schools may think, "Well, I'm doing fine, I'm getting Bs," despite the fact that they are in the bottom 5 percent of their class.

These students may very well deserve Bs relative to the people with whom they are being compared for college admissions, but having such a compressed range of grades leaves them without a true sense of how they are performing. There are many forms this dual reporting system might take, but essentially, it would amount to keeping the A–B range for grades when it comes to external reporting, but telescoping in on that and creating different categories within that small range for internal reporting.

WHEN TO REPORT

The last question to consider is when to report grades, and this is perhaps the simplest of the three. Of course grades are reported at the ends of terms, and how often this happens depends on the calendar used by that particular school. Yet these term-ending grades, if they cannot be changed (as is the case with most term-ending grades), are really useful only to external constituencies—policymakers, admissions offices, and employers. The more important time to report grades for students (and their parents) is during the course of a term. These reports, whether they are called midterm grades or indicator grades, are critical because they provide feedback while the term is in progress so that students may adjust and take steps to improve their performance before the summative grade—the one that will have an impact on their future—is reported.

How often students should be given indicator grades is a separate question. They should be getting constant feedback on their work, and if they are, these indicator grades are less necessary. However, the fact remains that students may have trouble translating the feedback they receive on their work, even if it does have a specific grade attached to it, into a summative grade. It may be ideal just to provide that feedback without a grade so that the focus is on the actual work and not the grade itself. However, many students, and more likely their parents, will want a more concrete measure of overall performance, and thus, an indicator grade somewhere around the halfway point of a term may be necessary.

CONCERNS REGARDING OPEN GRADE BOOKS

With all that this book has said about the importance of transparent grading practices and providing feedback for students, one might expect to find an argument in favor of open grade books—grade books that allow parents and students real-time access to all grades and a student's current average. On the contrary, there are a number of problems with this practice. Foremost among them is that constant access to grades will only serve to encourage a focus on grades—numbers, letters, and symbols—rather than actual learning. Many schools who do open their grade books feel that parents are entitled to this information. In fact, parents are entitled to the best education for their children, and the best education will encourage lifelong learning, something that an obsession with grades works against.

Furthermore, students and parents are also entitled to feedback on performance, and while they might think that grades equate to feedback, a number, letter, or symbol does not constitute specific, relevant, or useful feedback. A system in which parents have online access to all student work with grades and comments on it is much preferable. This would amount to an open portfolio, rather than an open grade book. Teachers should also keep parents updated with narrative feedback, particularly when there are some concerns or there is a drastic change in a student's performance. Giving parents access to student work and keeping them updated with narrative feedback will create genuine discussions about learning, not negotiations over grades.

Negotiations over grades is exactly what will happen if teachers open grade books, particularly since they provide access to numbers, letters, and symbols without any context. Teachers can expect to get flooded with e-mails and phone calls every time grades for a new assignment are posted. "Why did my son get this grade?" "Why did his average go down?" Parents could likely get the answer to the first question by looking at their child's work. As to the second question regarding a student's average, allowing access to this number in real time amounts to giving a summative grade before all of the data are collected. Again, this means parents see a number with no context and, in this case, one that could be quite misleading. Without information about the weighting of certain assignments, how many assignments are left, and whether or not teachers will eventually drop certain grades, a number can lead either to concern or complacency when neither is the appropriate response. All of this will lead to lots of unnecessary communication between teachers and parents, communication that will suck up valuable time that could be used in the service of learning.

It should be acknowledged that there may be a developmentally appropriate time for open grade books. Perhaps for younger students, at ages when grades are not viewed as such a high-stakes game (if such ages still exist), open grade books may serve a purpose without detracting from learning.

However, it remains true that access to numbers, letters, and symbols does little in the way of providing relevant, specific, and useful feedback about student learning.

Perhaps an electronic grade book exists that can alert parents when students are missing assignments, or when a student earns a grade that is substantially different—lower or higher (since it's always nice to pass along good news as well)—than his or her usual grades. This would serve the purpose of getting parents information they need and, if it was generated automatically, would actually save the teacher time. Above all, this system, unlike an open grade book, would not detract from learning through a focus solely on grades.

Part 3

Conclusion

Chapter 14

Shifting the Focus from Grades to Learning

The subtitle of this book is *Supporting Student Learning through a More Transparent and Purposeful Use of Grades*, and in concluding, it is critical to reemphasize these three elements of sound grading systems and policies— their transparency, their purpose, and their ability to support learning.

Transparency refers to the importance of clearly defining and articulating what our grades represent. This book has presented a range of possibilities for this, and while it has supported some of these possibilities more than others, the critical underlying point is that we must clearly define our grades, for without doing so, grades at best are misinterpreted, and at worst become meaningless.

We must also be clear about the purpose for which we are giving grades, and these purposes must be pedagogical in nature. It is worth reiterating the possible pedagogical purposes for using grades:

1. To generate data about students upon which to base decisions
2. To motivate students
3. To provide students with feedback on their work

Chapter 2 discussed the complexities and nuances of these purposes at length, but the underlying point is that we should not simply be giving grades just because that is part of the job or because that is what has always been done, but rather because doing so serves some pedagogical purpose.

Ultimately, the deciding factor in whether or not a grading system or policy is sound is whether or not they support student learning. Perhaps the largest concern here is the question of extrinsic motivation versus intrinsic motivation. The research cited in chapter 2 suggests that the very existence of grades as extrinsic motivators can inhibit deep and lasting learning. Thus, if we want to produce lifelong learners and not simply grade earners, and if what Susan Brookhart writes is true—"grades are not about what students *earn*; they are about what students *learn*"[1]—then we must make sure that students are not focused on grades at the expense of developing intrinsic motivation to learn.

What this means is that in the most effective grading systems, the grades essentially fade into the background, with the students' work and the specific feedback that they are given on it moving to the forefront. Hence, the essential point of this book is twofold: we need to use grades better—to demystify them and allow them to serve genuinely educational purposes, while at the same time de-emphasizing them so that the focus of teachers, students, and parents is the learning itself, and not the grades.

This book has gone to great lengths to show how to demystify grades, so now the question becomes, how does one de-emphasize them? This is not an argument that we should get rid of grades, for as shown earlier, they can support learning in a number of ways. A critic of grades might say that narrative feedback alone would be enough, and although there may be some validity to this argument, certain students need that grade as initial extrinsic motivation in the absence of intrinsic motivation. There is also something to be said for the ease of analyzing data in the form of numbers or letters in order to inform pedagogical decisions. Narrative reporting does not provide such data.

Thus, a de-emphasis of grades seems the middle path between grade obsession and no grades at all, both of which, as extremes, might be a detriment to learning. So what strategies can teachers employ to de-emphasize grades? A first step is simply not to talk about grades as often. Don't make comments such as "I'm really hoping to see higher grades on this next set of quizzes." Instead, say what you really want to see—"I'm really hoping to see a stronger knowledge of the chapter on the next set of quizzes," or whatever the learning is that you wish to see displayed. If a student asks you how he or she is doing in your class, don't respond with the grade. Instead, say exactly what the student is or is not doing well.

The same goes for written comments about a student. Don't start by writing, "I am pleased that Johnny earned an A for the fall semester." Instead, write, "I am pleased that Johnny displayed strong writing skills this past semester." The point is that—whether in speech or in writing—teachers should use the language of learning rather than the language of grades. Talk less about the labels we place on student learning and more about knowledge, skills, and habits of mind, and hopefully students will focus more on the latter than the former. After all, learning is not simply a means to an end; it is an end in and of itself.

Other ways of de-emphasizing grades include writing only comments on student work rather than actually putting a grade on it. This forces students to focus on the feedback provided as opposed to simply jumping to the grade and learning nothing from the teacher's assessment of the work. Students will undoubtedly want to know the grade, so you can require them to read your comments and/or the completed rubric and e-mail you stating what they think they earned based on your feedback and why. If they make a good-faith effort to do that, then you can tell them the grade. This has the added bonus of allowing a teacher to see, based on whether or not the student was able to determine the correct grade, if the feedback he or she was giving was clear. In the best of all possible worlds, students will begin to realize that the feedback is the grade, and no longer feel the need to ask for it.[2]

At this point, the reader may be wondering if there is a contradiction or at least a tension between increased transparency with regard to grades and a simultaneous de-emphasis of grades. This is not the case. In fact, what happens when we are more transparent about our grades is that students and their parents begin to see what they actually mean, and begin to focus, not on the grade itself, but on what's behind the grade—student learning.

NOTES

1. Susan M. Brookhart, "Starting the Conversation about Grades," *Educational Leadership* 69.3 (2011): 12.

2. For more on this practice, see Timothy Quinn, "A Crash Course on Giving Grades," *Phi Delta Kappan* 93.4 (2011): 57–59.

Twelve Steps to Improving Your Grading System

1. Establish a general definition for grades. This should explain what a grade is meant to represent.
2. Determine the purpose or purposes for which you will use grades.
3. Based on your general definition of grades and the purposes for which you will use them, determine what form your grades will take. Keep in mind that you may use different types of grades for different purposes.
4. Establish a policy for determining summative grades.
5. Decide whether or not you will include habits and behaviors in your grades.
6. Establish a policy for grading collaborative work.
7. Establish a policy for redos, retakes, and rewrites.
8. Decide when you will report grades and to whom you will report them.
9. Establish policies that help to encourage consistent grading practices.
10. Be sure that your grading system encourages a growth mindset in students and leaves room for intrinsic motivation.
11. Clearly communicate all elements of your grading system to all constituencies.
12. Constantly review your grading system and revise if necessary, while always keeping one question in mind—does it support student learning?

Acknowledgments

This book is the result of years of conversations about grading in many different schools, so it is impossible for me to list all of the friends and colleagues who have influenced my thinking on the topic. So I start with a big thanks to anyone who has taken the time to speak with me about grading over the years. I am sure that your ideas have found their way into this book in one form or another.

Undoubtedly, a number of the ideas in this book were spawned during the many meetings of the Westminster Teaching Initiative, and I am grateful to all of those who participated. A special thanks, though, to the regulars—Bill Sistare, Mark de Kanter, Charlie Griffith, Jill Loveland, Sara Deveaux, Dick Adams, Greg Marco, and Peter Ulrich—for contributing so much to those conversations.

Above all, I need to acknowledge the three great educational mentors in my life: Michael Cervas, Dennis Daly, and Todd Eckerson. Their diverse influences underlie all of my thinking about education. Todd especially deserves recognition for his direct contribution to the ideas in this book and because he was the first to encourage me to start writing about education.

Thanks go to Greg Williams, the former curriculum director at the Seoul International School. I don't know where Greg is now, but he was one of the first people to really get me thinking about curriculum and pedagogy in a systematic way.

My colleagues at the University School of Milwaukee also deserve recognition. I am sure if they read this book they will notice that I tested out many of these ideas at our curriculum and pedagogy discussions, which often could have been more aptly called "grading discussions." In particular, I would like to thank Nikki Lucyk for her help with the chapter on technology and Laura Klein for her assistance with the research.

113

I also need to acknowledge the numerous friends who have talked with me and, in some cases, have read parts of this book over the last year. Sam and Robyn Vierra, Regan and Amy Ross, Dan Hershel, Jon Downs, and Melissa Courtemanche are some of the best educators I know, and I thank them all for their help.

I can't thank my wife Sarah enough for her love and support during the writing of this book. In addition to taking care of our two children while I wrote, she found time to read and edit the entire book more than once, and her feedback was invaluable. I'll never forget the moment when she told me, after reading the first two chapters, that she had been "certain an entire book about grading would be quite boring, but this actually wasn't that bad."

There's no doubt that Sarah is the best teacher in our family. I thank her not just for her support and help with this book but for all the insights into effective teaching that she has given me over our many years together.

Annie and Connor, you didn't make the writing of this book any easier, but I'm glad you were around for it anyway. I promise that when you come home from school, I will only ask about your learning and not your grades.

I also want to thank Mark and Mickey Dalton for their help and support. During the process of writing this book, I realized how fortunate I am to have a father-in-law who is a publisher and a mother-in-law who doesn't mind watching my kids while I write.

Last, I want to thank my parents, who have always loved and supported me and always pushed me to learn. You encouraged me to strive for excellence in all of my endeavors and never measured that excellence simply by the grades that I earned.

Bibliography

Anderson, Karen. "Students Receive Fewer A's and Princeton Calls It Progress." *New York Times*, September 20, 2005. http://www.nytimes.com/2005/09/20/nyregion/20grades.html?_r=1&.

Babcock, Phillip, and Mindy Marks. "The Falling Time Cost of College: Evidence from Half a Century of Time Use Data." *Review of Economics and Statistics* 93.2 (2011): 468–478.

Bauerlein, Mark. "A Is for 'All Too Common': Rampant College Grade Inflation Is a Real Economic Problem." *New York Daily News*, July 24, 2011. http://www.nydailynews.com/opinion/common-rampant-college-grade-inflation-real-economic-problem-article-1.156828.

Binet, Alfred. *Modern Ideas about Children*. Flammarion, 1909. Reprinted in *Handbook of Competence and Motivation*, edited by Andrew Elliot and Carol Dweck. New York: Guilford, 2009.

Brookhart, Susan M. "Starting the Conversation about Grades." *Educational Leadership* 69.3 (2011): 10–14.

Deci, Edward L. "Effects of Externally Mediated Rewards on Intrinsic Motivation." *Journal of Personality and Social Psychology* 18 (1971): 105–115.

Deci, Edward L. "Intrinsic Motivation, External Reinforcement, and Inequity." *Journal of Personality and Social Psychology* 22 (1972): 113–120.

Dee, Jerry, and Michael Volpe. *Mr. D*. Canadian Broadcasting Company. Video, 2:01. December 16, 2011, http://www.youtube.com/watch?v=0fn_vAhu_Lw.

Dweck, Carol. *Mindset: The New Psychology of Success*. New York: Ballantine, 2006.

Flynn, James. *Are We Getting Smarter? Rising IQ in the Twenty-First Century*. Cambridge: Cambridge University Press, 2012.

Guskey, Thomas R. "Five Obstacles to Grading Reform." *Educational Leadership* 69.3 (2011): 17–21.

Harlow, Harry F., Margaret Kuenne Harlow, and Donald R. Meyer. "Learning Motivated by a Manipulative Drive." *Journal of Experimental Psychology* 40.2 (1950): 228–234.

Khan, Salman. *The One World Schoolhouse: Education Reimagined*. London: Twelve, 2012.

Kohn, Alfie. "From Degrading to De-grading." *High School Magazine* (March 1999): 38–43.

Lemann, Nicholas. *The Big Test: The Secret History of the American Meritocracy*. New York: Farrar, Straus and Giroux, 2000.

Pink, Daniel. *Drive: The Surprising Truth about What Motivates Us*. New York: Riverhead Books, 2009.

Quinn, Timothy. "A Crash Course on Giving Grades." *Phi Delta Kappan* 93.4 (2011): 57–59.

Rampell, Katherine. "A History of College Grade Inflation." *New York Times*, July 14, 2011. http://economix.blogs.nytimes.com/ 2011/ 07/14/the-history-of-college-grade-inflation/.

Rojstaczer, Stuart, and Christopher Healy. "Where A Is Ordinary: The Evolution of American College and University Grading, 1940–2009." *Teachers College Record* 114.7 (2012): 1–23.

Shenk, David. *The Genius in All of Us*. New York: Doubleday, 2010.

Sternberg, Robert J. "Intelligence Competence and Expertise." In *Handbook of Competence and Motivation*, edited by Andrew Elliot and Carol Dweck, 15–30. New York: Guilford, 2009.

Stiggins, Richard. "Assessment Crisis: The Absence of Assessment for Learning." *Phi Delta Kappan* 83.10 (2002): 758–765.

Tough, Paul. *How Children Succeed: Grit, Curiosity, and the Hidden Power of Character*. New York: Houghton Mifflin Harcourt, 2012.

Tough, Paul. "What if the Secret to Success Is Failure?" *New York Times Magazine*, September 14, 2011. http://www.nytimes.com/2011/09/18/magazine/what-if-the-secret-to-success-is-failure.html?pagewanted=all.

Wiggins, Grant. "A True Test: Toward a More Authentic and Equitable Assessment." *Phi Delta Kappan* 70.9 (1989): 703–713.

Wormeli, Rick. "Redos and Retakes Done Right." *Educational Leadership* 69.3 (2011): 22–26.

Index

The One World Schoolhouse (Khan), 60n6, 83–84
open grade books, 103–104

parents: grade inflation objected to by, 28; open grade books desired by, 103–104
pedagogy, 14
Pink, Daniel, 16–18, 19
Pride and Prejudice (Austen), 59
Princeton University, 29
punishments, 16
puzzles, 16–17

quantifications: evaluation's difference with, 8; grades as, 7, 8

rankings: definition of, 9; fixed mindset contributed to by, 23; grades as, 9, 14–15; number used for, 9; symbols used by, 9
redo justification memo, 57
redos: accountability for, 55–56; benefits, 59–60; case for, 55–56; classes with policies for, 59; creativity fostered by, 59–60; electronic portfolios allowing for, 81; grading, 57–58; implementing policy for, 56–58; innovation fostered by, 59–60; standards of, 60
report card, 98–99
reporting: audiences for, 100–102; behaviors, 99; to colleges, 101–102; dispositions, 99; grades, 97–104; student progress, 9–10; student skill level, 58; times for, 102
retakes: accountability for, 55–56; case for, 55–56
rewards: grades as, 17–18; intrinsic motivation diminished by, 16, 17
rewrites: accountability for, 55–56; allowing, 59; case for, 55–56; electronic portfolios allowing for, 81
Rojstaczer, Stuart, 27–28
rubrics: advantages of, 89–92; consistency encouraged by, 89–90; disadvantages of, 92–95; essays using, 41; expectations provided by, 90; feedback offered by, 90; grade and, 91; grading enabled by, 91–92, 93; inconsistency minimized by, 86, 87; for self-

assessment, 75–77; student progress tracked by, 90–91; students' limits placed by, 92; sum of parts of, 93; teachers' limits placed by, 92–93; using, 94–95

Scholastic Aptitude Test (SAT), 14
school districts, 87
schools: assessment disconnected from mission of, 61–62; colleges' needs served by, xiii–xiv, 11, 14; employers' needs served by, xiii–xiv, 11, 14
self-assessment: definition of, 75; after handing in work, 77; before handing in work, 75–76; possibilities for, 75–78; rubrics for, 75–77
Shakespeare, William, 59
Shenk, David, 29–30, 34
skit, 72
standardized measurements, 14
standards: of redos, 60; school districts mandating, 87; student performance defined by, 33
standards-based grading: feedback influenced by, 33; practical concerns, 32–33; student motivation diminished by, 33
Sternberg, Robert, 30
Stiggins, Richard, 24n12
student learning: definition of, 9; grades motivating, 15–20; inconsistency influencing, 84–85; student performance distinguished from, 9; student skill level distinguished from, 9
student motivation, 33
student performance: definition of, 9; GPAs reflecting, 51; grade inflation as alternative to, 28; standards defining, 33; student learning distinguished from, 9; student skill level distinguished from, 9; weighting toward most recent, 50
student progress: definition of, 9; reporting, 9–10; rubrics tracking, 90–91
students: bell curve influencing, 30; colleges learning about, 32; data ranking or sorting, 14–15; failure allowed to be experienced by, 53–55; grade inflation objected to by, 28;

About the Author

Timothy Quinn holds a BA from Amherst College, an EdM from Harvard University, and is currently a candidate for an MA from Middlebury College's Bread Loaf School of English. Timothy has taught English and moral philosophy at a range of independent and international schools, most recently Westminster School (Simsbury, CT) and the University School of Milwaukee (Milwaukee, WI), where he is currently the assistant head of Upper School. You can reach Timothy by e-mail at tjquinn6@gmail.com or follow him on Twitter at @TimothyQuinn6.

Made in the USA
Middletown, DE
12 May 2015